Wilson Reading System®

Instructor Manual

THIRD EDITION

by Barbara A. Wilson

Wilson Language Training Corporation

www.wilsonlanguage.com

Wilson Reading System® Instructor Manual

Item # WRSM12

ISBN 978-1-56778-052-9

THIRD EDITION

PUBLISHED BY:

Wilson Language Training Corporation
47 Old Webster Road
Oxford, MA 01540
United States of America

(800) 899-8454

www.wilsonlanguage.com

Printed in the U.S.A.

December 2013

Table of Contents

Introduction

The Wilson Reading System® was originally written for adults with dyslexia. This Third Edition is appropriate for elementary students as well as students beyond elementary grades who have not internalized sounds and word structure.

The Wilson Reading System directly and systematically teaches students how to fluently and accurately decode. It is unlike traditional phonics programs in that instruction is very interactive and multisensory. It also thoroughly teaches **total word construction** not just phonics. Students learn to encode (spell) as they learn to decode.

Since the first publication of the Wilson Reading System in 1988, many studies have been reported in the fields of reading and learning disabilities. Much of this research resulted from the commitment of the National Institute of Child Health and Human Development. It is worthwhile to contact NICHD for information (see Appendix for address). According to NIH, 75-80% of the special education students identified as LD have their basic deficits in language and reading.

Most people with reading disability demonstrate a core deficit in phonological processing (Bryan and Bradley, 1983; Liberman and Skankweiler, 1985; Wagner and Torgesen, 1987; Velutino et al., 1994). Moats and Lyon report that a key finding in research is the importance of code-emphasis instruction for students who do not automatically learn to read and spell. They emphasize that successful code-based instruction is not the "phonics" of old that was largely workbook oriented. Evidence shows when direct, systematic code-based instruction is skillfully implemented by a knowledgeable teacher, it is the most effective approach for problem readers (Moats & Lyon, 1996).

The ability to read and comprehend depends upon rapid and automatic recognition and decoding of single words. These studies report that the ability to decode single words accurately and fluently is dependent upon the ability to segment words and syllables into abstract constituent sound units (phonemes). According to these research projects, slow and inaccurate decoding are the best predictors of difficulties in reading comprehension.

These studies help to validate the necessity for programs such as the Wilson Reading System. The Wilson Reading System will teach students how to fluently and accurately decode. It is based on the multisensory language techniques and principles first described by Dr. Samuel Orton, Anna Gillingham and Bessie Stillman (Orton, 1937; Gillingham and Stillman, 1977). It is also based on successful experience with thousands of dyslexic students.

Third Edition - Dedication and Thanks

I dedicate this revision to the hundreds of teachers who have spent endless hours learning to teach students with dyslexia to read and spell with the Wilson Reading System. These teachers have taught me many things. Since the Wilson Reading Program was published in 1988, I have watched many "Wilson" lessons in settings of all kinds. I have learned what the teachers need to know in order to be successful, and I have seen many variations of Wilson activities. I thank these teachers for their dedication and determination to teach. I also praise them for their commitment to educate all students.

There are so many people I would like to acknowledge. First of all, my husband Ed has been my dedicated and selfless teammate. Without him, the Wilson Reading System and Wilson Language Training would never have been accomplished. Also close to my heart is Janet O'Connor, Executive Director, Wilson Language Training. She has been an inspiration to me all of my life, for she is my mother. I thank her deeply for all she has done.

The Wilson Language Trainers are all such talented individuals. They provide me with constant feedback and much of the revision emerged from this assistance. I thank all of them, especially the 'veteran' team: Maxine Goldman, Robin Carlo, Chris Ash, Nance Hoder, Linda Felle, Lisa Murphy, Nancy Hennessy, Kim Carr, and Barbara Green.

Two groups of people contributed to the "nuts and bolts" of this revision project. The Wilson Language Training staff were tireless in their effort. They are greatly appreciated for their extensive contributions. I thank Bert Baldarelli, Pauline Dupuis, Erica Lord, Tony Pepin and Elaine Wilson. In addition to the WLT staff, Reservoir Printing, with Ann Roseel at the helm, has done a fabulous job. Ann Roseel believed in the Wilson Reading System from its beginning days in 1987. I deeply appreciate Ann and her wonderful crew.

I also thank professionals in the field who unselfishly share their vast experience. In particular, I thank Margaret Rawson, Alice Koontz, Priscilla Vail and Diana Hanbury-King for providing words of encouragement. Their tireless dedication is such an inspiration to me.

Lastly, I greatly appreciate the extensive assistance given by Mary Pond, Margaret Logue, Linda Felle, and Cheryl Koki. Their editing has been invaluable.

To the Instructor

The English Language is fascinating! So rich in vocabulary...so able in expression. Though English is complex, it is also quite beautiful. The more I study and learn, the more I love the language.

This reading and spelling program is sure to teach you interesting points about words that you've never even realized. I hope you find it to be a rewarding journey. Your students will come to understand our language for the first time - you may see it like you've never seen it before.

Please enjoy words. So many people say phonics instruction is boring. This may be true if a teacher merely drilled sounds and rules. However, this program is actually a study of the total 'construction' of the words in our language...and, it is far from boring. It is truly exciting to learn!

Many people have not acquired adequate reading and spelling skills due to a learning style that demands multisensory, structured, language techniques. They need to be directly taught decoding skills that go beyond the phonics skills normally presented. These people must learn the sound / symbol relationships in a multisensory manner. Equally important, they need to be taught syllable types and "word construction" rules. Most phonics programs stop short after sounds are taught. Many students, however, need to learn word parts so that multisyllabic reading and spelling become manageable.

I now believe I can teach any child or adult with at least low average cognitive ability and intact vision and hearing to accurately decode. I hope to share this with other teachers who search for solutions so that they, too, can reach and teach their students.

Practice. Be thorough. Children deserve to learn how to read. Those beyond childhood deserve an apology and then our full commitment to make amends for their prior lack of learning.

Note: Throughout this manual, the pronouns **he** and **him** are used - please understand that these indicate both genders and were chosen merely for fluency in writing style!

Who Is This System Designed For?

The Wilson Reading System is designed for students who struggle with decoding and spelling.

WRS directly teaches the English language. It is appropriate for students who have not internalized the sound and syllable system for reading and spelling. Students will benefit from the program whether or not they have been diagnosed as dyslexic.

This program will greatly benefit:

- Students with dyslexia
- Students unable to decode accurately:

    Slow, labored readers who lack fluency

    Students who may know many words by sight, but have difficulty reading new words and "nonsense" syllables

    Students who often guess at words

- Students able to speak and understand English, but not read or write it (such as ESL students)
- Poor spellers
- Students unsuccessful with other reading programs or who still have "gaps" in their decoding and/or spelling

A common misconception is that students who have poor auditory skills should not learn phonics. Students thought to have poor "auditory" skills very frequently lack **adequate linguistic / language skills**. They actually require **direct**, **multisensory** teaching in order to master skills needed for reading and spelling. When language is presented in this manner, they learn how to gain mastery over their weakness.

This program follows a ten-part lesson plan that addresses decoding, encoding, fluency, vocabulary and comprehension. This manual provides detailed instruction for parts 1-5 with an emphasis on word study, and parts 6-8 with an emphasis on spelling. Guidance for planning lesson parts 9-10, as well as weaving vocabulary and fluency throughout the lesson, is provided on the Wilson Academy® / Intensive Learning Community and in Level I and II Certification training.

It is important for parents and teachers to understand that Wilson Reading System students learn the English language step-by-step. Initially, they may be unable to make the transition to non-controlled text. As they progress in the program, more and more may be done independently by the students. Most often, students need to complete Steps 1 - 6 before significant reading and spelling progress can be documented by standardized testing. However, progress should be clearly evident on the WADE if a student is responding to the program. At that time, students will begin to have success reading non-controlled text in addition to the Wilson materials. In the meantime, things should be read to students until they can independently decode.

Getting Started

Wilson Language Training **recommends its specific training** for teachers so that the program is properly implemented. If using this program without training, we suggest the following:

- Read this Manual thoroughly.

- Write lesson plans and **practice**.

- Utilize Wilson Academy® / Intensive Learning Community online support. Register at www.wilsonlanguage.com/register. (The prerequisite is the WRS Introductory Workshop.)

- Work 1:1 before implementing in group settings.

- If possible, observe classrooms with Wilson certified teachers.

To Begin

1 Read the Introduction to this manual and briefly review the first three Student Readers. Be sure to gain an overall understanding about the concepts taught in the first three steps.

2 Prepare a teacher binder and a student notebook.

Teacher Binder

Copy the following pages from the Appendix of this manual:

- The Scope and Sequence

- Approximately twenty lesson plans to get you started

- A wordlist chart (for each student)

Student Notebook

Each student creates a personal notebook as he progresses through the program. This notebook is a reference to be used at any time. The notebook should be set up by tabbing it into 5 sections: sounds, syllables, spelling rules, sight words, and vocabulary.

Additionally, each student will need a composition book for his Dictation work (Part 8 of the lesson).

3 Administer the Wilson Assessment of Decoding and Encoding (WADE). Select a starting point: 1.1 or 1.3 according to student pretesting. See **"Where to Begin"**

4 Read the Substep instruction (1.1 or 1.3) in this manual thoroughly, prepare a lesson and practice it.

Where To Begin

Pretesting

The WADE should be administered to the student before the program is initiated. Follow the directions in the User's Guide. Standardized reading and spelling tests are helpful and certainly recommended.

Students must not omit any concepts taught in this program. Therefore, all students must begin in Step 1. Some students begin in 1.1 and others begin in 1.3. Most students beyond elementary grades begin in 1.3.

Some students start at Step 1.1

Students who do not know the consonant sounds must begin here, as should nonreaders and students reading below grade 2 level. You are going to move slowly with students starting in Step 1.1. Let the student feel confident with each new sound. If the Student Readers do not provide enough practice, create additional materials using only appropriate words.

Most students start at Step 1.3 in the Student Readers

Students begin in 1.3 if they are weak in decoding or spelling but have a reading score at grade 2 level or above. Older students often begin here if they know most of the consonant sounds even if they do not know the short vowel sounds. All short vowels can be introduced with keywords, then practiced to mastery.

Those beginning in 1.3 will learn to master the sounds for consonants and short vowels. They will begin to learn sound segmentation, an essential component of the program. Some students will need to use both real and nonsense words, while many others will focus mainly on the nonsense words in Steps 1 & 2. Sentence and story reading can be used to break established guessing habits.

For students starting in step 1.3 who know very few words, even by sight, initially use the real words. When the real words are mastered, use the nonsense words. Establish phoneme segmentation skills and develop smooth sentence and story reading within each Substep - move slowly.

Those students starting at step 1.3, who easily recognize real words, can move as quickly as possible through Steps 1 & 2. Use the nonsense wordlists and be sure the student can blend and segment the sounds adequately.

How Fast To Move

The initial lessons with a student are so important! You need to find a balance between proceeding too slowly and going too fast. Experience will answer this question best! All students must move somewhat slowly at first. It is essential to set a firm foundation. The student must become automatic in the use of sounds and the use of phoneme segmentation for reading and spelling.

Do not proceed until each Substep is mastered. Mastery is achieved when a student reads approximately 95% of the real and nonsense words correctly, without prompting, and spells approximately 75% - 80% of the words.

The pace will vary throughout the program. Some Substeps will require several lessons while many others may take only one or two sessions to complete. The pace must be individualized to each student's performance.

Student Initiation

It is essential to approach older students in a positive, upbeat manner. They have often experienced so much failure, they do not believe they can learn to read.

Do not be apologetic for using Sound Cards! Make it clear that these sounds are the 'core' of the English language and they must be mastered for adequate reading and spelling. It is effective to instruct students in a businesslike manner, yet bring humor and enjoyment to the lesson.

Tell the Student

You know many words by sight, but it is impossible to memorize all the words in our language! Many words you don't know, and right now you can only guess at them.

Words follow a reliable system, and once you know this system you will be able to figure out new words easily. You need to learn this system in detail, so you won't have to guess at new words. Explain that this program is a thorough study of **word structure**.

Words in English are comprised of sounds. Letters represent sounds (show the student the Sound Cards). These sounds are combined into word parts called syllables.

You are going to learn the sounds and syllables (there are only six kinds of syllables). You will learn these gradually until you know all of them. We will start with several sounds and the first type of syllable. At the end of the twelve steps, you will be able to figure out almost any word that you see.

The student may ask how long the program will take. Tell him that you can't honestly say. It varies, depending upon many factors: attendance, past knowledge, what else is happening in the student's life, his independent work, degree of language difficulty, etc. Most students complete the program in two to three years.

Tell the student that an important aspect of the program is substantial practice for each new concept. It is more important to master each step than to hurry through it.

How To Introduce New Sounds

Whenever a new sound is introduced, use the following procedure:

1 Present the Sound Card to the student:

Tell the student the name of the letter(s), the keyword on the back of the card and the sound that the keyword represents. Explain that the keyword is a clue to the sound. Tell the student to listen to the first sound in the keyword.

For example, tell the student that /**m**/ is at the beginning of man and that keyword will help him remember the sound. Then have him repeat, say letter name-keyword-sound: "**m** - **man** - /**m**/." This sequence helps the student use the keyword to get the sound. It also ends with the sound so that the student can **easily** use it. Don't say "**m** says /**m**/ as in **man**". This sequence is less effective.

*Be sure that the student does not add an extra vowel sound after the consonants. **B** - /**b**/, not /**bŭ**/, etc. This is a very common error and must be avoided by the instructor as well as the student!*

2 As each new sound is learned, it must be entered into the student's notebook. The Manual instructions will direct you to do this. The student must memorize the keyword and sound. Eventually, when the Sound Card is presented to the student, he should be able to say the letter name, keyword and sound without prompting. As a new sound is taught, the Sound Card should be added to the student's known sound pack to be drilled at each lesson. Mastered sounds can be gradually eliminated from the pack to be reviewed only periodically.

3 The Sound Cards are coded to the Substep in which the sound is taught (see below). Some letters have more than one sound. **Do not teach all the sounds and keywords at once!** Be sure to teach each sound and keyword in the Substep that is indicated on the card. If more than one sound has been taught, the students should give all the taught responses for each card.

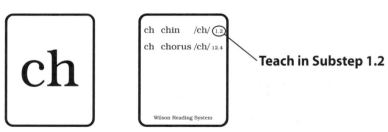

4 The peach cards are vowel sounds, including vowel digraphs, diphthongs and r-controlled vowels.

The ivory cards are consonant phonemes including consonant digraphs.

The green cards are sound combinations, as opposed to phonemes ("welded" sounds).

Syllable Instruction

The Wilson Reading System teaches word construction according to six types of syllables. The instructor must understand these before beginning instruction. These syllable types will be gradually taught to the student. Sounds are introduced only as they relate to the syllable.

1 Closed Syllable (Steps 1-3)

- · Ends in a consonant and only has one vowel
- · The vowel in a closed syllable is short
- · Real words: **up**, **hat**, **ship**, **last**
- · Nonsense: **strup**, **plish**, **em**

2 Vowel-Consonant-e Syllable (Step 4)

- · Has the vowel-consonant-e combination
- · The **e** is silent
- · The first vowel has a long sound
- · Real words: **bike**, **ape**, **stove**
- · Nonsense: **ploke**, **pute**

3 Open Syllable (Step 5)

- · Ends with a single vowel (this might be the only letter in the syllable)
- · The vowel has a long sound
- · Real words: **I**, **be**, **shy**, **hi**
- · Nonsense: **spo**, **fla**

4 Consonant-le Syllable (Step 6)

- · Contains a consonant-le
- · This syllable occurs at the end of a word
- · The **e** is silent (it is present only because every syllable needs a vowel)
- · Only the consonant and the **l** are sounded
- · Real words: **cradle**, **little**, **bubble**

5 R-Controlled Syllable (Step 8)

- · Contains a vowel combined with an **r** (**ar**, **er**, **ir**, **or**, **ur**)
- · The vowel is neither long nor short; its sound is controlled by the **r**
- · Real words: **start**, **fir**, **hurt**, **art**
- · Nonsense: **flir**, **shar**, **erst**

6 Vowel Digraph/Diphthong "D" Syllable (Step 9)

- · Contains a diphthong or vowel digraph
- · Real words: **beat**, **feel**, **eight**, **new**
- · Nonsense: **bloit**, **plaw**, **stey**

Syllable Marking

Six Types of Syllables

1 **Closed Syllable:** d r ĭ p
c

2 **Vowel-Consonant-e Syllable:** b r ā k e̸   or   b r ā k e̸
e   v-e

3 **Open Syllable:** s h ē
o

4 **Consonant-le Syllable:** t ā b l e̸
o   -le

5 **R-Controlled Syllable:** b(ar)k
r

6 **Vowel Digraph/Diphthong "D" Syllable:** t(ow)n
d

To divide words into syllables, underline or 'scoop' them. Do not slash between syllables.

cat nip   or   **catnip**   not   **cat/nip**

Scope and Sequence (see Appendix)

The structure of the language is taught in a very systematic, cumulative manner. Concepts are taught step-by-step, following a specified sequence. First, closed syllables are mastered in one-syllable words (Steps 1 and 2).

Steps 1 and 2 strongly emphasize phonological awareness with segmenting and blending of phonemes up to six sounds. Finger tapping is used for analyzing spoken words into phonemes for spelling. It is also used for blending sounds for reading. Then closed syllables are combined in Step 3 to form multisyllabic words (such as **catnip** and **Atlantic**).

Steps 4 and 5 introduce long vowels in syllables with the vowel-consonant-e and open syllables. Step 6 introduces suffixes in unchanged basewords and the consonant-le words (such as **dribble**).

Steps 1- 6 exclude sound options and complex spelling rules in order to establish a solid foundation to build upon. Steps 7-12 present more complex rules of the language including sound options, spelling rules, and morphological principles.

Necessities for Program Success

1 Multisensory Instruction

The student must learn the new concepts with the manipulation of Sound Cards, Syllable Cards and Suffix Cards. This helps him understand the word construction.

The lesson plan format must be followed for each lesson. This includes the multisensory approach needed for success.

2 Repetition

Never teach a concept, then move on to others, and leave the taught concept behind. In other words, constantly incorporate taught concepts into the lessons. Review by questioning the student while he looks at words. Include spelling words from previous steps. Go over the student's notebook often.

3 Sound / Syllable Segmentation

The program is based on phoneme (smallest unit of sound) segmentation and syllable segmentation. The ability to break a word into individual sound units must be **directly** taught with the Sound Cards and sound tapping. The student must master both sound and syllable segmentation. To read and spell, he needs the ability see and hear each syllable and each sound within a syllable. For this reason, Steps 1 & 2 are essential, even for readers who can read and spell the real words in these steps. Beginning in Step 3, syllable segmentation is emphasized. This too must be directly taught with Sound Cards and Syllable Cards.

4 Reading and Spelling Control

The Wilson Reading System provides practice in both reading and spelling with **controlled** text. This is key for student mastery. The words presented to the student will contain only elements of word structure that have been directly taught. When students master Steps 1-6, it becomes essential to practice reading non-controlled text with supervised guidance.

5 Pacing / Mastery

A student will become a proficient reader *if and only if* the pacing through the program is appropriate. The student must become fluent in one Substep before progressing to the next.

Instruction

One-to-One Instruction

It is highly recommended that you first learn to teach the Wilson Reading System with one student. It is best to identify a student who needs this approach and work 2-3 times per week with him. In this way, you become familiar with the essential lesson plan procedures as well as the language concepts. With proficiency, you will then be successful in a group setting.

Group Instruction

The Wilson Reading System (WRS) can be taught in small groups. When it is implemented as a remedial reading program, the groups should be limited to 3-5 students. The program is sometimes taught with remedial groups as large as 10-12 students, but the teacher must be highly trained. (Wilson certification is recommended.)

Proper student placement is the most important factor for successful group instruction. Students must be pretested and grouped according to similar scores on **word attack** and **spelling** measures. **Total** reading scores and comprehension scores should not be used for placement.

For example, in an 8th grade class, 19% of the students may have reading scores 3-4 grade levels below their current placement. These students must not be automatically placed together. The reading scores must be analyzed. Some of these students may in fact be fluent decoders but have poor comprehension. These students should not be in a Wilson Reading System class.

Students with similar word attack scores should be grouped together. The 8th grade class may have some students with very limited decoding ability and others with some decoding ability but many gaps. These students need to be in separate groups.

8th Grade Students - Word Attack Percentile Scores	
Group 1	between 0 - 15%
Group 2	between 16 - 30%*

* Just Words is ideally suited to students with test scores in the 15th-50th percentile range.

The pacing for each of these two groups will most likely be very different.

Vocabulary Level

A Level vs. B Level

Substeps throughout the WRS contain both A and B Level vocabulary (see Student Readers and the Dictation Book).

A Level

A Level words and sentences are appropriate for:

- Elementary grade students
- ESL students
- Older students with limited vocabulary

Recommendations

Students using primarily the A Level words may read B Level **wordlists** for additional decoding practice or to replace nonsense word reading. These students should be told that the words are real words, but the meaning need not be discussed. These words can be revisited for meaning at a later date when the student(s) are ready. These students **should not** read B Level sentences or stories if the vocabulary is above them, since the meaning is essential when words are in context.

For additional reading, controlled materials written for younger students are available from other publishers. It is essential to use controlled text that coordinates with concepts taught in WRS. **SRA** Basic Reading Series, Books A-B coordinate with Step 1, Book C with Step 2, and Book D with Step 3. See Appendix for additional resources.

B Level

B Level words and sentences are appropriate for:

- Students beyond elementary grades with advanced vocabularies

B Level vocabulary ranges from somewhat difficult to extremely difficult. It will be necessary to discuss vocabulary and at times be selective depending upon student(s).

Recommendations

B Level students should be introduced to new concepts with A Level vocabulary wordlists and sentences. When A Level words are easily decoded and spelled, B Level vocabulary can be used, as appropriate.

Groups

Students within the same group may vary in level of vocabulary. Thus, use A Level with some students and B Level with others. Concepts should be taught and reviewed with the entire group of students using the A Level words.

WRS Lesson Plan Outline

BLOCK	LESSON PART	LESSON ACTIVITY	TIME	BLOCK EMPHASIS

Word Study

1 — Sound Cards Quick Drill

MINUTES
1:1 🕐 2-3
GROUP🕐 2-3

Block Emphasis:
Phonemic Awareness
Decoding
Vocabulary
Single Word Accuracy/ Automaticity
Phrasing / Prosody

2 — Teach & Review Concepts for Reading

MINUTES
1:1 🕐 5
GROUP🕐 5

3 — Word Cards

MINUTES
1:1 🕐 3-5
GROUP🕐 5-10

4 — Wordlist Reading

MINUTES
1:1 🕐 5
GROUP🕐 5-10

5 — Sentence Reading

MINUTES
1:1 🕐 5
GROUP🕐 5

Spelling

6 — Quick Drill in Reverse

MINUTES
1:1 🕐 1-2
GROUP🕐 2-3

Block Emphasis:
Spelling
Proofreading
Vocabulary
High Frequency / Sight Words

7 — Teach & Review Concepts for Spelling

MINUTES
1:1 🕐 5
GROUP🕐 5-10

8 — Written Work Dictation (Sounds, Words, Sentences)

MINUTES
1:1 🕐 15
GROUP🕐 15-20

Fluency / Comprehension

9 — Controlled Text Passage Reading

MINUTES
1:1 🕐 10-15
GROUP🕐 10-15

Block Emphasis:
Guided Reading
Fluency
Vocabulary
Comprehension
Visualization
Oral Language Skills

10 — Listening Comprehension / Applied Skills

MINUTES
1:1 🕐 15-30
GROUP🕐 15-30

Lesson Plan Scheduling

A Wilson lesson moves at a quick pace with constant interaction between the teacher and the student. The student is often practicing the same skill but in a different way. The skill taught for decoding in the first half of the lesson is then taught for encoding in the second half of the lesson.

One-to-One Instruction

When teaching the Wilson Reading System 1:1, Parts 1 through 8 can be done in 45-50 minutes, and Parts 9 or 10 in 10-15 minutes. This is dependent upon the student, however. Parts 1 through 8 may require a full hour. Parts 9 and 10 must then be done during an alternately scheduled time. The final two parts of the lesson plan can actually be entire lessons on their own.

When working 1:1, schedule a minimum of two lessons per week. This is the absolute minimum. Students will progress more quickly, of course, if scheduled five days per week.

Note: Some adults are successful with one hour-long lesson per week. This prolongs the length of training but in some circumstances it is necessary.

Group Instruction

In group lessons, it is impossible to complete an entire lesson unless students are scheduled for a double period block of time. The following schedules provide a framework for group instruction.

45 - 60 Minute Lessons			
	Block 1	Block 2	Block 3
Monday	Parts 1 - 5		Part 9
Tuesday	Parts 1, 2	Parts 6, 7, 8	Part 9
Wednesday	Parts 1 - 5		Part 10
Thursday	Parts 1 , 2	Parts 6, 7, 8	Part 10
Friday	Parts 1, 2 Select: Block 3 (Part 10), Charting, Fluency Drills, Spelling Test or Wilson Games		

75 - 90 Minute Lessons			
	Block 1	Block 2	Block 3
Monday	Parts 1 - 5	Parts 6, 7, 8	Part 9
Tuesday	Parts 1 - 5	Parts 6, 7, 8	Part 9
Wednesday	Parts 1 - 5	Parts 6, 7, 8	Part 10
Thursday	Parts 1 - 5	Parts 6, 7, 8	Part 10
Friday	Parts 1, 2 Select: Block 3 (Part 10), Charting, Fluency Drills, Spelling Test or Wilson Games		

Parts 1 Through 5 - Emphasis on Decoding

1 Sound Cards: This includes a "quick drill" of the phonemes with the teacher showing a Sound Card and the student(s) naming the letter(s) and corresponding sound(s). Keywords are always used with vowels and as needed with other sounds.

2 Teach / Review Concepts for Reading: Blank cards and letter cards are used to teach phoneme segmentation and blending (initially). Students are taught to segment sounds using a finger tapping procedure. Beyond Step 2, Syllable and Suffix Cards are used to teach total word structure. Every lesson involves this manipulation of cards to teach word structure and practice reading.

3 Word Cards: Skills learned in section 2 of the lesson are applied to reading single words on flashcards. Review words are included in the stack of cards presented.

4 Wordlist Reading: Skills are applied to the reading of single words on a controlled wordlist in the Student Reader containing only those elements of word structure taught thus far. In 1:1 lessons, the student is charted daily for independent success. In group lessons, students are charted before progressing to the next Substep. The list changes with each lesson so that students never memorize the list.

5 Sentence Reading: Word attack skills are applied to reading within sentences. All sentences contain only the elements of word structure taught thus far.

Parts 6 through 8 - Emphasis on Encoding

6 Quick Drill (in reverse): Letter formation is taught as needed. Every lesson includes a phoneme drill with the teacher saying a sound and the student identifying the corresponding letter(s).

7 Teach / Review Concepts for Spelling: Initially, the student spells words with phoneme cards and blank cards. Students apply the finger tapping procedure to segment sounds for spelling. Beyond Step 3, students use Syllable and Suffix Cards. Students spell words using the cards to sequence sounds, syllables and word parts.

8 Written Work: Sounds, single words and sentence dictations are included. The teacher dictates sounds, words and sentences that are controlled; they only contain the word structure elements directly taught thus far. The student repeats the dictation prior to writing. Sounds and words are spelled orally before they are written. A formal procedure is followed for independent sentence proofreading.

Parts 9 and 10 - Emphasis on Reading Comprehension

9 Passage Reading: The student silently reads a short passage with controlled vocabulary containing only the studied word elements. The student retells the passage in his own words linked to visualization of the passage. The student then reads orally.

10 Listening Comprehension / Applied Skills: In this part of the lesson, the teacher reads "non-controlled" text to the student. The student uses visualization and retelling to develop comprehension skills at a higher level than current decoding.

Lesson Plan Procedures

The lesson plan has ten parts: Parts 1-5 emphasize decoding and Parts 6-7-8 emphasize encoding or spelling. It is best to do the encoding and decoding in the same lesson. Part 9 emphasizes fluent reading and comprehension of controlled passages. Part 10 emphasizes listening comprehension and application of skills. Use a blank lesson plan (see Appendix) to plan each lesson.

Part 1: Sound Cards Quick Drill (2-3 minutes warm-up)

· Always do vowels: letter-keyword-sound

· Other sounds: be selective - include new, trouble spots, rotate for review. Say letter-keyword-sound or just the letter and sound.

Every lesson starts with a quick drill of sounds. This takes approximately 2-3 minutes. It is a warm-up to get your lesson going. Use this part of the lesson to get those sounds drilled into the students' heads!

Do the vowels in every lesson. For the vowels, students always say the letter name, keyword and sound (**a** - **apple** - /ă/). Initially, the teacher should model the sounds as needed and encourage students to use their notebooks.

Do the consonants at the beginning, but as students know their consonants, there is no need to do every consonant in every lesson. Be selective: do the new consonants and include the trouble spots. Use keywords for consonant sounds as needed. Otherwise, students simply say the letter name and the sound (**m** - **man** - /**m**/, or simply, **m** - /**m**/).

Part 2: Teach & Review Concepts for Reading (approximately 5 minutes)

· Manipulate cards to practice for reading

· The teacher makes words with cards in order to teach word structure. Depending upon the step, cards to manipulate include Sound, Syllable and Suffix Cards.

Throughout the program, all concepts are taught with cards. At the beginning of the program, use the Sound Cards. As you progress, you will also use Syllable Cards, and still later in the program, you use Suffix Cards. If you are at the same Substep for a long time, you still do this part: *you either teach or reteach using different examples every single lesson.*

Work on a table surface or use a magnetic board, manipulating magnetized cards. After you teach a concept with the cards, make additional examples to practice, and use questioning techniques to reinforce.

It is with the questioning that students start to internalize the concepts, and it is with practice that students begin fluently decoding.

Part 3: Word Cards (3-5 minutes)

· Moves from the presentation of words in parts (Part 2 of lesson plan) to the presentation of whole words. Give many examples to practice new skill (weave with questions).

· Always include review cards from previous Substeps.

In the third part of the lesson you present entire words. The following examples highlight how Part 3 differs from Part 2.

In Part 2 of the lesson, you use Sound Cards to present `sh` `i` `p`.

In Part 3, you use Word Cards to present `ship`.

In Part 2, you use Sound Cards to present `i` `n` `d` `e` `x` or Syllable Cards `in` `dex`.

In Part 3, you use Word Cards to present `index`.

WRS Word Cards provide a sampling of every Substep. Re-discuss what you introduced in Part 2 as you present the words as a whole.

Periodically weave with questioning. Students should read words as fluently as possible. Students can track with a finger or pencil point under the letters as they read the word.

Make additional cards as needed:

· If you are in the same Substep for awhile

· To target trouble spots

· To target specific vocabulary

1 If you are in the Substep for a long time, the WRS sample Word Cards become meaningless. Select the words from the Student Reader to make additional Word Cards. Students may also help with this activity.

2 Make Word Cards to target any trouble spots. For example, if in 1.3 a student has difficulty with **b** / **p**, make many Word Cards to practice:

`lap` `lab` `cob` `cop` `tap` `tab`

3 Lastly, in each Substep, select 3 or 4 words to target for vocabulary. For older students in 1.3, for example, you may select the words **vim**, **posh**, **thug**, and **wit**. Students add these words to the **Vocabulary Section** of their notebook. Have them write a sentence using the word and draw a picture, if possible. Put these words on Word Cards in order to review them in subsequent lessons.

Part 4: Wordlist Reading (from Student Reader) (approximately 5 minutes)

· Practice: select approximately 5-6 words, targeting trouble spots

· Discuss current concepts and weave with questions

· **Chart**: select 15 words from current Substep (the top or bottom of a page). This group of words should not be the words practiced and should not be the same words charted in the previous lesson. Here the student applies taught skills independently.

· First response counts, chart errors, discuss the errors with the student.

· Use as guide for progression: do real...then nonsense.

Charting a Student When Working 1:1 (See the Wordlist Chart in the Appendix)

Chart daily. Select a wordlist page in the Student Reader that is appropriate for the current Substep.

Before charting the student, have him practice 5-6 words. Don't practice the same words that you will chart. Select words with the student's trouble spots and discuss. Weave with questions. Encourage the student to use his notebook, tapping, etc.

The reason for charting is to determine a student's independent application of the decoding skills. Do not assist or correct until this list is completed. Encourage the student to use his notebook, tap, or take his time, but the first thing said aloud to you counts. Your goal is to get the student to apply what you are teaching and to help him break guessing and impulsive habits. The charting provides motivation.

At the top of the column, write the Substep information (1.3 - R) to indicate the type of wordlist charted. Have the student read the words on the given list and record student errors in boxes, starting at the top (#15) and working down. Record errors only.

The student can color the remaining boxes after reading all 15 words. The result is a bar graph demonstrating progress. Review errors with the student and discuss patterns of errors that reflect "trouble spots." Plan subsequent lessons to target these areas.

Within a Substep, chart real words until the student can fluently read 15/15. In subsequent lessons, chart nonsense words (if provided) until the student fluently reads 13-15 correct. From lesson to lesson, do not re-chart the same list of words. Chart a different list from the same Substep.

Charting Groups

Chart periodically. Most lessons, however, simply read and discuss words. Select a student to read a column of words. When the majority of the students seem proficient, plan an entire lesson to chart students individually. **Each** student should have a personal chart.

Progress to the next Substep when the majority of students in the group can fluently read the words and correctly chart 13-15 words (real and nonsense). Students should be able to self-correct errors with your questioning guidance.

Part 5: Sentence Reading (from Student Reader) (approximately 5 minutes)

- Goal is to complete 10 sentences

- The student reads silently, then orally, with assistance given as needed.

- Reading for meaning is essential. Use pencil for tracking and fluency (the teacher models).

Select any sentence page in the Student Reader from the current Substep. Sentences will only contain words with the concepts taught. Any words with untaught elements appear within a bar at the top of the page. If the student has difficulty with any of these barred words, just tell him the word. With the other words, use questioning techniques to help the student as needed.

The student should read the sentence silently, then aloud. He can use his notebook or tap out any word, if necessary. Many students are impulsive and read orally, rather than silently first. You need to train them to slow down and read independently, applying skills.

The sentences must be read for meaning. You need to establish, right from the beginning, that reading means decoding the words and understanding what the words mean.

Penciling

Modeling of fluency is important. Work with fluency by modeling and have the student reread a sentence after you model it. Have him read with a pencil in his hand. Some students have been told that it is babyish to use their finger or a pen. You have to counteract that and tell them that there is a neurological link which helps connect them to the text when a pen point or finger is used.

Penciling is used to help maintain focus whenever a student reads the wordlists, sentences or stories. The student should track the sentence with the point of a pencil or retractable ball-point pen. Sentences can be scooped in phrases to assist with fluency.

The fish on that dish is hot.

Initially, this should be modeled by the teacher and then imitated by the student.

Part 6: Quick Drill in Reverse (1-2 minutes)

- Use the "What Says?" page in the Dictation Book to plan.

- Spread out Sound Cards.

- The teacher says the sound. The student repeats the sound, points to card(s) that have the graphemes representing the sound, and answers.

- The student can also make the letter(s) with his index and middle fingers on the table surface or in sand to add a tactile-kinesthetic reinforcement.

- Teach letter formation as needed (see Handwriting in the Appendix).

Part 6: Quick Drill in Reverse (continued)

Initially, spread Sound Cards out on the table and ask the student to repeat the sound and find the card(s). Be sure he repeats the sound before answering. This "echoing" of the sound helps you know that he heard it correctly, and it will help him process it. The student should also name the letter (not to just point to it). An additional reinforcement is a tactile / kinesthetic reinforcement: the student can make the letters on the table with two fingers while saying the letter name and the sound of the letter.

As you progress in the program, be sure to add new sounds. Also, this can eventually be done orally without the Sound Cards displayed. There is no need to do every sound taught. Dictate new sounds, review some previously taught sounds, and target "trouble spots".

Part 7: Teach & Review Concepts for Spelling (planned from Dictation Book) (approximately 5 minutes)

- The **student** manipulates cards and spells orally.
- Initially use Sound Cards, then blank cards. Beginning in Step 3, use Syllable Cards and Suffix Cards.
- The teacher dictates the word and the student repeats it. With one-syllable words, the student taps sounds, finds letters and orally spells word while tapping.
- With multisyllabic words, the student names and spells one syllable at a time, using Syllable Cards. Sounds are tapped only as needed.
- Words with a suffix: use Suffix Cards - the student names and spells the baseword first and then adds the Suffix Card.

In Part 7 of the lesson, (the exact opposite of Part 2 of the lesson) the **student** makes the words. You dictate a word, and the student repeats the word, taps it out, finds the letters, and spells it orally. In Steps 1 and 2, students must segment the sounds and then identify the letter(s) that go with each segmented sound. This is done with finger tapping as explained in the Substep instructions.

Blank cards can be used as well as Sound Cards. The blank cards must represent the sounds accurately. For example, the student selects white-peach-white cards to represent the word **shop**. The student then names the letters that correspond to each card: **sh - o - p**.

Eventually, instead of pulling down individual Sound Cards, you will have the student pull down Syllable Cards and Suffix Cards. Once you move to multisyllabic work, students spell one syllable at a time. This is fully described in Step 3.1.

Part 8: Written Work Dictation (Sounds, Words, Sentences) (approximately 10-15 minutes)

This should be done in the composition book. The page should be set up by the student.

	Date:				Date:
1			S		
2			1		
3			2		
4			3		
5					
R	N		1		
1	6		2		
2	7		3		
3	8				
4	9				
5	10				

Sounds (5)

Teacher says sound:

- · Student repeats
- · Student answers orally then writes
- · Student says answer again while writing

Words

- · 5 real/ 5 nonsense/ as needed...2-3 sight words

Always select words from current, as well as previous Substeps.

Teacher says word:

- · Student repeats
- · Student taps sounds (/**m**/ - /**a**/ - /**p**/) and then taps again, naming letters (**m**, **a**, **p**)
- · Student writes word, naming letters while writing
- · Student rereads list of words

Teacher directs student to "mark up" list (e.g. underline digraphs, circle suffixes, etc.)

Note: see **Sight Word Instruction** for Sight Word Dictation procedure.

Sentences

- · 2-3 sentences

Teacher dictates the sentence:

- · Student repeats
- · Student writes independently

The teacher then guides the proofreading process:

- · Reread dictated sentence
- · Have the student check for capitalization and punctuation
- · Have the student check spelling of all words by tapping and scooping syllables
- · Use questioning to lead to corrections
- · Student rereads sentences

This is a teaching time, not a testing time. The student always repeats dictations of sounds, words and sentences.

Use the Dictation Book to plan this part of the lesson. Select **sounds** from the "What Says" page, select **words** from current and previous Substeps and select **sentences** from the current Substep.

With sounds and words, the student answers orally before writing. Make corrections with guidance, then have the student write. Note errors on your lesson plan. With sentences, the student writes first, then makes corrections with your guidance. The student should proofread each sentence immediately after writing it. Guide the student through this process after each sentence is completed by student.

The student should work independently when writing sentences. If he asks for help, tell him to check his notebook, tap it out, or if it is a "barred" word, tell him how to spell that word. When he has the entire sentence written, you re-dictate as the student points to the words on his paper. This checks to make sure he has all the words. Then ask, "Do you have a capital at the beginning and a punctuation mark at the end?"

Next, lead the student through the sentence to proofread it. Teach him to look at the words while he taps out sounds. Have him proofread it, even if it is perfect. Proofreading one-syllable words means: tap out words to be sure all sounds are represented by letters. Proofreading multisyllabic words means: scoop the words into syllables and circle suffixes. Use questioning to lead the student to the corrections. You want him to find and fix his errors with your guidance, and then eventually without your guidance.

Part 9: Controlled Text Passage Reading

·   Select "controlled" passage

·   Student reads silently (uses pencil for tracking)

·   Student visualizes passage - replays - retells

·   Teacher must model visualization and retelling process

·   Student reads orally

Dyslexic Students require practice, practice, practice in order to become fluent decoders. The more dyslexic, the greater the need for practice.

The purpose of Part 9 is essentially threefold:

1   To increase the student's automaticity of application and reading fluency

2   To develop comprehension using visualization

3   To develop oral expressive language skills

Fluency / Automaticity of Application

Students need to become proficient readers. Instruction will be fruitless if the students remain unable to decode fluently. In order to achieve this, most students will require lots of practice. Initially, this needs to be limited to 'controlled' text. As students learn skills for decoding, they need to read passages that contain only the taught elements. For this purpose, the following material can be used:

Students Using A Level Vocabulary

·   A Level Stories (WRS Student Readers)
·   Other phonetically controlled text as appropriate (see Appendix)

Students Using B Level Vocabulary

·   A and B Level Stories (WRS Student Readers)
·   WRS Stories for Older Students by Jay Brown and Travels with Ted by Jay Brown

Procedure for Students to Follow when Reading Controlled Stories

Have the student read the title and discuss it. Write down any vocabulary word that seems challenging. Have the student read the word and discuss its meaning. The student then reads the story silently. The penciling technique should be used at this time (this is described in Part 5 of the lesson plan).

The student should visualize a picture in his mind while reading. Use questions to get the image of the story in the student's mind. Go through the passage, sentence by sentence, helping to create a movie in the student's head. The student then retells the story in detail, linking the retelling of the passage to his mind's visual image.

Clarify and discuss the passage as needed. The student then reads the passage orally, using the penciling technique. Use questioning techniques to correct any decoding errors. Tell the student the "barred" words at the top of the page. Model fluency as needed and have the student reread. Explain to the student that this part of the lesson is important to practice fluency and visualization. Repeated readings can be done with the same story. The story can also be sent home to be read and practiced for homework. Audio taping the story can be helpful. Tape the story, modeling fluency. Have the student listen and follow controlled text. The student can then practice fluency and audiotape himself.

Part 10: Listening Comprehension / Applied Skills

Read non-controlled text to student

·   Read to the student

·   Help with visualization

·   Student replays, then retells

Student reads non-controlled, decodable text

·   See page 30 for procedure

Select appropriate passages from literature (including poetry), a newspaper, or magazine. Read to the student. The student doesn't need to follow along. He should listen and transfer the words into a picture in his mind. Stop and help him get a picture in his mind. Describe what you 'see' or have him explain what he 'sees' with leading questions such as, "What is the man wearing?"

Model visualization and retelling. When the student retells the story he doesn't need to remember the specific names. He might say, "A man traveled on a ship..." etc. He doesn't need to say, "Mr. Sanchez traveled on a boat called the Santiago Express."

Initially, do short segments at a time. Read. Work with the student to develop imagery and have him retell that segment, linking the retelling to the image. Lengthen the segments as the student develops his skill.

Questioning / Weaving

Questioning for Skill Reinforcement and Mastery

Questioning techniques should be used throughout each lesson. Concepts will be directly taught to students with cards in parts 2 and 7 of each lesson. In Part 2, cards will be used to teach decoding skills, and in Part 7, cards will be used to teach encoding or spelling skills. After teaching the current concept with cards, make new examples and use questioning techniques to assure that the student has understood. This also provides repetition of concepts so that they become mastered.

For example, teach the difference between a blend and a digraph using Sound Cards in Part 2 of the lesson:

Explain the difference: consonants in a digraph stay together to make **one** sound, whereas consonants in a blend **each** get sounded individually and are then blended together. After teaching this with cards, make new examples such as:

Ask questions such as:

- "Where is the blend?"
- "Where is the digraph?"
- "How many sounds in the blend?"
- "How many sounds in the digraph?"

The 'teach, then question' techniques create a success-oriented lesson. Weave the questioning throughout the lesson. Note: **weave** - do not overkill! Weave review questions as well as current ones. At the end of each Substep you will find suggestions for questions pertaining to that Substep.

Important: avoid word retrieval questions such as "What is this called?" pointing to the blend. Dyslexic students have significant word retrieval difficulty. These questions usually frustrate them and make it seem as though they are not learning, when indeed they are learning but have trouble recalling the specific word.

Questioning for Error Correction

During a lesson, expect students to make errors. Due to the "controlled text" used in the program, you can lead the student to make corrections with questioning techniques. Do not tell the student the word when misread unless it contains untaught elements. If a student misreads the word **chop** as **shop**, for example ask, "Is there a digraph in that word?" (yes), "What letters are in the digraph?" (**ch**), "What is the keyword for **ch**?" (**chin** - student can check personal notebook for assistance), "tap out the word, using /**ch**/ sound" (**chop**). You lead the student through a series of questions to make the corrections. The questions can be answered, and thus, again, you are creating a positive, success-oriented lesson.

Targeting "Trouble Spots"

If a student has significant difficulty with a particular sound, such as distinguishing **e** for **i** when spelling, target that area in your lessons. During each lesson, be aware of the kind of error(s) that are made during the various parts of the lesson. Diagnosing, then targeting trouble spots is very important. Below is an example of a typical student error in the program. The teacher needs to diagnose the problem, discuss it with the student, and then teach the student. The teacher then must provide practice so that the student becomes better and better at overcoming the area of difficulty. Address this area of difficulty in subsequent lessons in all the parts of the lesson, but especially Parts 2, 3, 7, and 8.

Error

cap read for **cab** or **lab** read for **lap**

Diagnosis of Problem

b / p error

This error is common, especially at the end of a word.

Discussion and Teaching

Teacher should point this error out to the student. It is helpful to explain that **b** and **p** are both formed on the lips. Make each sound and have the student make each sound to see and "feel" how they are made. Now hold your hand to your throat. You can feel a vibration with the /**b**/ sound but not with the /**p**/ sound. /**b**/ and /**p**/ are a voiced and unvoiced pair of sounds (see Appendix for list of voiced and unvoiced consonants). This means that they are very similar in formation - both labial or lip sounds - but they differ slightly (/**b**/ is produced with a resonance in throat and /**p**/ is not). Explain that these two sounds can be easily confused. Use the keywords and teach the student to "double check" the sound in 2 ways:

1 with the help of the keyword

2 by "feeling" the difference in his throat

Practice

In Part 2 of subsequent lessons, the teacher should make words with **p** and **b**. These words should be selected from the current Substep (or previous Substeps). Thus, the teacher makes words with cards:

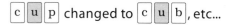 c u p changed to c u b, etc...

The student should reference the keyword in his notebook and feel his throat while practicing these words. **B** and **p** Word Cards should be made by the teacher or student for **Part 3** of the lesson. Words with **b / p** can be highlighted within sentences. The teacher can dictate similar words in **Parts 7 and 8** of the lesson. Thus the student has numerous opportunities to practice applying technique to help him overcome his "trouble spot."

Student Progress / Pacing

It is **critical** to set a secure base. Even if the student seems to have little problem reading / spelling words in Step 1 and Step 2, do not move too quickly. There are a lot of critical concepts to master and if you go too fast, these will not be secure. Also, the student needs to practice some tapping (segmenting of sounds) even if they can read, and it is **critical** that they become good at segmenting the sounds for spelling.

Student Progress

At the beginning of the program, take the time to establish the good habits that you will need for success. Students must begin:

- Breaking the guessing habit and using skills (tapping, notebook, keywords)
- Reading independently (silently) before orally reading
- Reading fluently and accurately with pencilling as needed
- Breaking down words to spell rather than trying to spell from memory
- Spelling orally *before* writing, and then again when writing
- Writing as neatly as possible
- Proofreading independently after writing a word or a sentence
- Retelling stories in sequence using visualization

Pacing from One Substep to the Next

Fluency is the goal. This requires internalization of the concept along with ease of application. This program is cumulative. If taught correctly, with mastery at each step, the students become readers. **Severe** dyslexics might always be slow readers, but they will be able to access the print. However, the majority of students needing multisensory structured language teaching are not so severe. In all of my experience with nonreaders who have struggled for many years, I have met only a handful that I would classify as extremely disabled. By far the majority are indeed dyslexic, but they are not so severe. Being dyslexic, they are not intuitive language learners. They need specific help to learn written language. With that help, however, these individuals can learn to read and write. And with much practice, their reading and writing can become more and more fluent.

For a new teacher of multisensory language, correct pacing through the steps of the program is one of the most difficult aspects to learn. It is essential to work with students until a Substep becomes easy for them. Explain this to your students. Tell them that you want to be sure they can almost do it in their sleep. They may be anxious to move ahead but the upper steps will not be successful without mastery of each step. Do not move on to the next Substep if they are not yet reading the words without "tapping" them first or sounding out each sound. Move on when they can read across the word and nonsense syllables. It is okay if a student periodically gets "stuck" on a word and must tap it out in order to get it. However, this must only happen once in awhile.

Progression to the Next *Substep* Depends Upon:
- Charting at least 15/15 (real) *and* then 13/15 (nonsense) words without tapping
- The ability of a student to self-correct any reading or spelling error with assistance given by the teacher with questioning techniques
- Fluency of sentence and story reading
- Spelling (at least 75% accuracy)
- Understanding / mastery of concept taught

Posttesting

At the end of every step, students must pass a posttest before progressing to the subsequent step. The posttest lesson plan is found in the Appendix. In addition to passing the test, the student should be fluently reading the Substep sentences and stories. If the student is not yet fluent, spend time modeling and practicing with the penciling technique. You can tape record sentence pages and stories. The student can listen and follow along with a pen or pencil point. The students can "echo" you or the tape recording, scooping with his pencil. The student can then practice the sentences and stories until fluency is achieved.

1   **Posttest for Reading** (found on the last 2 pages of Student Readers)

    ·   Chart Real Words (A and/or B)

    ·   Chart Nonsense Words

These lists contain words and nonsense words from each of the Substeps.

The student should chart at least 14/15 on each list. The student must self-correct any error. If the student is unable to self-correct, determine what is the "trouble spot" and work more on this before moving to the next step.

2   **Posttest for Concepts**

A copy of the Posttest page from the Student Reader can be made for the student to "mark up" as directed on the posttest page of the Student Reader.

3   **Posttest for Spelling** (use Dictation Book to plan)

Dictate 15 real and 5 nonsense words, selecting approximately 2-3 words from each Substep. The student can use his/her notebook to reference sounds and rules. The student does not spell orally first when taking the posttest but he may tap out the words, as needed. A student may progress with up to 5 errors on the spelling posttest as long as he is able to self-correct any error with guidance.

Sight Word Instruction

Certain words in the English language need to be memorized because they do not follow the "system" of the language. These words can be called sight words because they need to be memorized. Luckily, the number of words that need to be learned by memory is very limited. Some sight words are quite common. These are important for the student to master.

Sight words to be memorized by the students have been organized according to Wilson Substeps. For example, **was** and **wha**t are sight words that do not follow rules taught in Step 1.3. Thus, these words appear on the 1.3 sight wordlist. The sight words are listed at the end of the **Rules Notebook**. There are both A and B level vocabulary sight words.

Select sight words to present to students. The starred (*) sight words are essential. Select other words according to the student's needs and ability.

Sight Word Instruction (continued)

Students should create a sight word dictionary. This is one of the 5 sections of their personal notebooks. This sight word dictionary is a reference. This section of the notebook should be set up alphabetically: A, B, etc. Any sight word introduced to students should be written into the dictionary on the appropriate page. Students can refer to this dictionary at any time.

Teachers should select no more than 3 sight words at a time. These sight words are then introduced to student(s) to be mastered for reading and spelling. As sight words are mastered, additional sight words can be added. Mastered sight words should be kept in the sight word flashcard pack and should be constantly reviewed.

If a student knows how to read and spell a sight word, it can be added to his dictionary but the following procedure will not be necessary.

Reading: Part 3 in Lesson (Word Cards)

Make a large flashcard to teach the reading of an unknown sight word. These should be made with large, traceable letters on an index card. If the student knows cursive writing, do the word in cursive in order to help the fluency of tracing. The sight words should not be mixed in with the other Word Cards. Sight words should be presented to students as words that can't be tapped out. Initially, the teacher should read the word and have the student repeat. The student should trace and name letters and read the word again.

Spelling: Parts 7 and 8 in Lesson

Teach the spelling of selected sight words during the **preparation for written work**, Part 7 of the lesson plan. Use the flashcard and explain to the student that this word must be **memorized**.

1 Present the sight word on a flashcard and have the student read it. If he is unable to read it independently, read it to him.

2 Point out any clues to help memorization.

3 Have the student say the word, trace the letters, and say the word again.

4 Have the student write the word with 2 fingers on the table: say the word, write with fingers while spelling orally and say the word again. Sand trays, etc. can also be used.

5 Have the student use gross motor memory, with arm extended (elbow **straight**, 2 fingers pointed), eyes closed. Tell him to visualize the word as he says the word and spells it while making letters in the air. The student can pretend to write the word with purple or red paint coming from his fingers. He can write graffiti (in his mind) on the wall in large letters.

6 During written work, include sight word dictation, until mastered, then periodically. Be sure to do these **separately** from other words. Possibly 5 real, 5 nonsense, 2 sight words, if time allows.

7 Select sentences with the sight word(s).

Reading and Writing Fluency

Students must practice reading and spelling in order to become proficient. Students need to read, read, read. Students need to write, write, write.

Reading

Steps 1 - 6

Initially, a dyslexic student will have very limited success reading non-controlled text. Practice to automaticity with 'controlled' text is essential. Thus, throughout the first 6 steps of the program, students should read and reread the wordlists, sentences and passages provided and other available controlled texts (see Appendix for resource list for younger students) until fluency is achieved.

During this time, students should listen to good literature as well as factual text. Thus, teachers and/or parents must read to the student(s) from 'non-controlled' sources. Books on tape can be a source of listening as well. However, success with these depends upon the individual's overall skill with auditory comprehension of language.

As students progress in the program, introduce non-controlled, decodable text when they can read the text independently with 95% accuracy (see below for guidelines).

Beyond Step 6

Practice with 'non-controlled' decodable text must begin if it has not yet been introduced. It is essential and should be done under supervised guidance.

Hours and hours of "practice" must occur in order for more and more automaticity to happen. The student should read with someone familiar with the WRS. Thus, the person can 'feed' the student words with untaught elements. For example, if the word **partial** appears in the text when the student is in Step 7, he can be told the word if unable to decode or determine it from context since it contains word elements taught in future steps. The teacher should guide students with questioning techniques if the unknown word contains taught elements.

Writing

Students must be encouraged to write. Process writing, creative writing, and journal writing are very appropriate. Initially, students should not be held accountable for spelling. As progress is made in the WRS program, students must be held accountable for the proofreading and correction of any taught patterns.

Formal instruction in spelling should be limited to the controlled words in Wilson and a limited number of sight words. Other lists of words to be memorized will merely provide a source of frustration. Dyslexic students should not be given random words to memorize for spelling.

Step 1

At the end of this step, students should know:

- All short vowel sounds, definition of a vowel
- All basic consonant sounds, definition of a consonant
- The definition of a digraph, sounds of digraphs **ck**, **sh**, **ch**, **wh**, **th**
- How to blend three sounds into a real word or nonsense syllable
- How to segment and spell words with three sounds
- The nasalized **am** and **an** sound combinations
- **ll**, **ss**, **ff** spelling rule
- How to add the suffix -**s** to a 3-sound word, **s** can say /**z**/
- Definition of a baseword and suffix

Step 1 sets a foundation for all Wilson students. For some students, it may be the first time they read and spell words at all. For many others, it may be the first time they begin to realize how to decode and encode rather than read and spell words entirely by memory. They will begin "breaking the guessing habit."

Some students will need to begin in Step 1.1 (non-readers and students with a reading level below grade 2). Many students begin in 1.3. Students must master the fluent blending of three sounds in both real words and nonsense syllables. They must also become independent at segmenting 3-sound words and then associating the letter(s) to correspond to each segmented sound for spelling. Students will learn basic skills and procedures to be used throughout the program. They will learn some terminology as well. Lastly, they will begin the study of "total word structure" with the introduction of the simple suffix -**s**.

1.1   What to Teach

- Sounds for the consonants **f, l, m, n, r, s, d, g, p, t**

- Sounds for the vowels **a**, then **i** and **o**

- Sound tapping process for blending and segmenting two and three sound words

- Reading and spelling words with 3 sounds: with **f, l, m, n, r** and **s** in initial position, short vowels **a**, then **i**, then **o**, and the letters **d, g, p** and **t** in the final position

Additional Materials Needed

- Sound Cards: **f, l, m, n, r, s, d, g, p, t** (ivory) **a** (peach) then in future lessons, **i** and **o** (peach)

- 1.1 Word Cards

- Step 1 Student Reader and Student Rules Notebook

- Student Workbook 1A (optional)

Note: Throughout entire program, use Teacher's Manual, Dictation Book and Rules Notebook to plan and execute lessons.

PART 1

a

Spread out the Sound Cards: **f, l, m, n, r, s, d, g, p, t** and **a**. Tell the student that the **a** is on a peach card because it is a special letter called a **vowel**. The rest of the letters are all consonants (point to the cards). Ask the student to name the letters as you point to each one. If he can name them, tell him that you will begin working with these letters. If he cannot name them, tell him that you will be teaching him these letters and how to make words with these letters. In the beginning lessons, do only Part 1 and Part 6 of the lesson until the student becomes more and more able to do these two without your modeling. Then do the entire lesson.

Begin the student's Sound Section in the notebook. Write the word **consonant** at the top of the page and tell the student the word. Explain that he will make a notebook to learn the consonant sounds. One at a time, hold up the consonant card, say the letter name and tell the student the sound, "**f** says /**f**/." Tell him that a **keyword** will help him remember the sound. Have him repeat the keyword, **fun**, and then listen for the /**f**/ sound. Have him repeat the keyword, **fun**, and then listen for the /**f**/ sound at the beginning. Hold the sound, /**f**/ when saying **fun**. Have the student repeat after you, **f** - **fun** - /**f**/.

Do all the consonants, using as many pages as needed. You make the letters large enough for the student to trace. Then have the student draw a picture of the keywords. Put the word **vowel** at the top of another page and start the vowel page with **a**. The student should draw an apple and practice saying **a** - **apple** - /ă/. Be sure to teach the student how to use the keyword **apple** to get the sound /ă/ by extending the first sound: (/ă/) **a........apple**. Model this.

When all the 1.1 sounds are entered (not **i** and **o**) review the notebook. You trace each letter, say the keyword while pointing to the picture, then say the sound. Make the student repeat, tracing and pointing as you did.

PART 2 Explain that letters are blended to form words. Use Sound Cards to make the words that appear in the Student Reader. For example:

Teach Sound Tapping for Reading

Say sounds separately, then blend together. Tap your thumb to your fingers over each Sound Card, while saying the sound. Use the index finger to thumb for /**m**/, middle finger to thumb for /**ă**/, and ring finger to thumb for /**t**/. Then blend the sounds and name the word, as you drag your thumb across your fingers beginning with the index finger. Have the student do this. Explain that they can say sounds, while tapping and blend them together to make words. Do the 1.1 words only! Teach the student to hold onto the first sound, into the vowel sound, and hold the vowel sound into the last sound. Model until the student can do words without you modeling. Start by changing the last consonant:

 to to s a p

Follow the wordlist guide in Student Reader One.

PART 3 WRS Word Cards provide a small sample. You or your student should make a Word Card for **every** 1.1

 word after you do the words with Sound Cards in Part 2: | mat | | sat |

These cards will then be used to practice decoding fluency. Students can tap these initially. Eventually model dragging your finger under the word as you say each sound, blending it into the word. Have the student do this after you model it.

PART 4 Use the 1.1 wordlists in the Student Reader. Have the student read the words, tapping as necessary.

 Eventually the student must be able to do the wordlist without tapping. Model this by dragging your finger under the words as you read them. Have the student succeed with one list before progressing to the next. Before doing the next 1.1 list of words, present the words with Sound Cards (lesson plan Part 2) and Word Cards (lesson plan Part 3).

PART 5 There are only three sentences for each wordlist in 1.1. These sentences can be written on cardboard

 strips. **The rat is mad.** You can write the sight words in red ink. These are the words that are between bars at the top of the page such as **The**, **is**, etc. Tell the students these words. They cannot be sounded out. The student should read the sentence, using his finger to track under the words. Model fluency. The student can then read the same sentence in the Student Reader. Again, tell him the sight words as needed and model fluency, always using your finger or pencil/pen point while reading the sentence. The student can also draw a picture of the sentence on the cardboard strip (front or back).

PART 6 Spread out the Sound Cards: **f**, **l**, **m**, **n**, **r**, **s**, **d**, **g**, **p**, **t** and **a**. Have the student refer to his notebook as

you dictate sounds. Say a sound such as /**m**/. Ask the student to repeat the sound. Then have him look in his notebook to find the letter that says /**m**/ using the keywords as a guide. Assist as needed. When the correct letter is identified, have the student find the corresponding Sound Card. The student should then trace the letter in his notebook and say **m** - **man** - /**m**/. Next cover the letter and have the student make the letter on the table surface from memory, using two fingers while saying **m** - **man** - /**m**/. This can also be done in a sand tray.

This provides kinesthetic / tactile reinforcement of the letter formation. Link the letter formation with the letter name and its sound by saying **m** - **man** - /**m**/ while making the letter. Gross-motor movement can also be used here to reinforce the formation. Extend the student's writing arm (left or right). His elbow and wrist should be straight and two fingers should point out to write the letter. A large letter is then drawn in the air. Again, say **m** - **man** - /**m**/. Do this as needed to teach the letter formations. If the student knows the correct letter formations, do this periodically but not every time.

PART 7   **Teach Sound Tapping for Spelling**

 For Spelling, use the Sound Cards to teach sound tapping for segmentation skills. With the Sound Cards, form an appropriate 1.1 word. For example: |m| |a| |t|

Tap thumb to finger above each card as the sound is said. Count the number of taps (three). Re-explain that there are three separate sounds in the word **mat**. Take away the Sound Cards. Tell the student to try to picture the three cards in his mind, even though they are no longer on the table. Say /**m**/, /**ă**/, /**t**/, and tap thumb to fingers for each sound. Now tap **mat** again, this time saying the letter names as finger taps thumb. Take the cards back out and explain that to spell words, you tap out the sounds and then correspond each tap with the letter that makes the sound. Repeat this procedure with other appropriate spelling words. Spread all the 1.1 Sound Cards out. Orally dictate a 1.1 word without first getting the corresponding cards. Tap out sounds and have student repeat. Then have the student find the corresponding cards and place them on the table. Next, dictate a 1.1 word and have the student try tapping out the sounds and finding the letters. The student should then re-tap the word, this time saying the letter names as he taps.

PART 8   See the explanation of this part of the lesson in the Introduction. The student should use an appropriate composition book. Young children beginning the program in 1.1 should have a composition book with lines to guide letter formation.

Follow the procedure to dictate five sounds and five words. To do the sentence dictation in 1.1, you write sight words into the student's composition book, leaving a space for the 1.1 words in the sentence. For example, write '**The** _____ **is** _____.'

Then dictate the sentence ('**The rat is mad.**') and have the student fill in the 1.1 words needed to complete the sentence. Be sure to point out and discuss the capital letters and punctuation marks.

PART 9   Step 1.1 does not have any controlled stories. These begin in Step 1.3.

PART 10   Read good literature to the student for listening comprehension and enjoyment. Other people (parents, friends, other teachers) can also help with this effort.

Notes / FYI

Gradually teach the **i** and **o** sounds as the student is ready to progress to these new sounds. Add these into the student notebook on the vowel page, make Word Cards, and follow the same procedures used with the **a**.

1.2   **What to Teach**

- Sounds for the letters **b**, **sh**, **u**, **h**, **j**, **c**, **k**, **ck**, **e**, **v**, **w**, **x**, **y**, **z**, **ch**, **th**, **qu**, and **wh** (gradually introduced)

- The definition of a digraph

- How to read and spell words with three sounds and short vowels (including words with digraphs)

Additional Materials Needed
- Sound Cards for sounds listed above (gradually introduced)

- 1.2 Word Cards

PART 1

Follow the same procedures used in Step 1.1. Gradually introduce sounds as indicated in the Student Reader. Do the entire lesson plan as described in 1.1. The student should master one group of sounds and words before progressing to the next. Include review and current words in Parts 2, 3, 7 and 8.

Teach the concept of **digraph** when you introduce the **sh** sound. Show the student the **sh** Sound Card. Tell him that even though there are two letters on this card, they stay together to make one sound: **sh** - **ship** - /**sh**/. It does not say /**s**/, /**h**/. Since it is one sound, it will only get one tap.

Tell the student that **q** is a '**chicken letter**' - it refuses to go anywhere without its friend, **u**. **Qu** is never in a word alone. The **u** in this situation makes no vowel sound. We refer to **qu** as a digraph as well, although technically it is not since it has two sounds /**kw**/. We tap it with one tap and it is on one card: **qu** - two letters that make the sound /**kw**/.

Notebook Entry
(Sound Section) Add each new sound to the student notebook as it is introduced. Begin a new page in the student's notebook called Digraphs. As you progress through this Substep, add the other digraphs to this page (**ck**, **ch**, **th**, **wh**).

PART 2

Be sure to use Sound Cards to teach and practice words. Teach how to tap words with digraphs. Teach the **sh** digraph first. Use Sound Cards to make the word sh o p.

This word will get three taps since it has three sounds. The /**sh**/ sound gets one tap.

PART 3

Use the WRS Word Cards as appropriate. Make additional Word Cards. Mix new Word Cards with the previously taught "stack."

PART 4   **PART 5**   Follow the procedures for 4 and 5.

PART 6 Be sure to include the new sounds as they are taught. Use the "What Says?" page in the Dictation Book as a guide.

 PART 7 Follow the procedure used in 1.1. When **c** and **k** are taught, tell students to use **c** at the beginning of a word unless you tell them otherwise. Likewise, after **w** and **wh** have been taught, tell the student to begin words with **w** unless you tell them otherwise. When **ck** is taught, tell the student to use this at the end of words (after a short vowel). For practice, dictate words and have them find the corresponding cards. The student should always orally spell the word after pulling down the cards. Have the student tap again, naming the letters that correspond to each tap.

 PART 8 Be sure to include review sounds and words. Select appropriate sentences following the gradual introduction of sounds. Continue to use the 1.1 procedure for sentence dictation, providing the sight words for the student prior to dictating the sentence.

 PART 9 **PART 10** Follow the procedures for 9 and 10.

 Notes / FYI
Wh and W
The sound of **wh** has changed over time. Many people currently pronounce **wh** the same as **w**, as opposed to /**hw**/. This sound can be practiced as /**hw**/, but if the student is asked "What says /**w**/?" the answer should be **w** or **wh** since this is how they will most likely hear it pronounced by most people.

 Helpful Hints / Activities
See 1.3 for good ideas.

1.3   What to Teach

· Sounds for short vowels, consonants, digraphs

· Sound tapping process for blending and segmenting sounds

· How to read and spell words and nonsense syllables with three sounds

Note: If the student began in Step 1.1, this Substep provides additional words, sentences and stories for practice. Nothing new is presented. Read the lesson plan procedures in the introduction. Now begin doing the full lesson plan as outlined.

Additional Materials Needed

· Sound Cards **a, e, i, o, u** (peach) and **b, c, d, f, g, h, j, k, l, m, n, p, qu, r, s, t, v, w, x, y, z, wh, ch, sh, th**, and **ck** (ivory).

· Step 1.1, 1.2 and 1.3 Word Cards

· Step 1 Student Reader and Student Rules Notebook; Student Workbook optional

In the very first lesson, explain the Wilson program to the student. Then introduce the Substep sounds and start the notebook (Part 1 only). Start the short vowel page (**a, e, i, o, u**). Have the student draw keyword pictures beside each vowel. Explain digraphs and start the digraph page. The student can make pictures for these as well. Start the consonant page. The student can list all consonants, but only troublesome and unknown consonants need keywords with pictures. In subsequent lessons, do **all** parts of the lesson following the procedures outlined in the introduction. Specific guidelines are provided below for unique parts of the lesson.

PART 1

Teach the sounds below, using the procedure described in the **How to Introduce New Sounds** section of the Introduction.

Vowels
a, e, i, o, u (short only). These are vowels; the sounds are unobstructed. The sound can be continually extended without lips or tongue getting in the way. Teach keywords for the vowels, even if the student already knows the sounds. Extend the vowel sound at the beginning of the keyword: /**a**/........**pple**.

Consonants
b, c, d, f, g, h, j, k, l, m, n, p, qu, r, s, t, v, w, x, y, z. Explain that if a letter is not a vowel, then it is a consonant.

Tell the student that **q** is a 'chicken letter' - it refuses to go anywhere without its friend, **u**. It is never in a word alone. The **u** in this situation makes no vowel sound. We refer to **qu** as a digraph as well, although technically it is not since it has two sounds /**kw**/. We tap it with the tap and it is on one card: **qu** - two letters that make the sound /**kw**/.

If consonant sounds are already known, a student need not memorize keywords for each of them. Many students know the consonants and need not use keywords. Teach keywords for any unknown sound. **Be sure students clip consonant sounds** (/**m**/ not /**mŭ**/).

Digraphs

th, **ch**, **sh**, **wh**, **ck**. Explain that these consonants 'stick together' to form one sound, even though there are two letters. That is why they are on one card. They are not separated. **Sh**, for example, will not say /**s**/, /**h**/ - these letters stay together to say /**sh**/.

Notebook Entry

(Sound Section) Begin student notebook. Create a short vowel page, a digraph page and consonant page(s). Student(s) must draw a picture for keywords (vowels, digraphs, and any unknown consonants).

PART 2

Teach Sound Tapping for Reading

Explain that letters are blended to form words. Form 1.3 words with Sound Cards (use Student Reader to select words). Use only the letters and sounds taught to form words with three sounds. Make the word **mat**: |m| |a| |t|

Say sounds separately, then blend them together. Tap thumb to finger over each Sound Card, while saying the sound. Use index finger to thumb for /**m**/, middle finger to thumb for /**a**/, and ring finger to thumb for /**t**/. Then blend the sounds and name the word while dragging your thumb across fingers, starting with the index finger. Have the student do this. Do many words to practice. Digraphs get **one** tap. /**m**/ - /**a**/ - /**sh**/. If the student knows how to read these words, explain that it is important that they demonstrate that they can also segment the sounds and, thus, "tap" them.

PART 3

See **Lesson Plan Format** instructions in this manual.

Also, spread out cards (make additional Word Cards using Student Reader). Have students find and read cards as directed. For example: find any card that begins with a digraph, find any card that has the vowel sound /**ĕ**/.

PART 4   **PART 5**   Follow the procedures for 4 and 5.

PART 6

Spread out Sound Cards. Arrange so digraphs are together and others are alphabetical:

a	b	c	d	e	f
g	h	i	j	k	l
m	n	o	p	qu	r	s
t	u	v	w	x	y	z

wh	ch	sh	th	ck

Note: In subsequent lessons, students can help arrange cards, practicing alphabetical order. To prepare for dictionary skills, letters can be arranged in four rows since dictionaries can be divided into four quadrants **a** - **f**, **g** - **l**, **m** - **s** and **t** - **z**. The **f**, **l**, **s** and **z** end the rows. This will help in Substep 1.4 when the "bonus" letters are learned.

Use the "What Says?" page in the Dictation Book to plan this part of the lesson. Ask the student, "What says /**m**/?" etc... Follow the Lesson Plan Format.

PART 7 **Teach Sound Tapping for Spelling**

Spread out the Sound Cards. Use them to teach sound tapping for segmentation skills. With the Sound Cards, form the word **bat**: b a t

Tap thumb to finger above each card as the sound is said. Count the number of taps (three). Re-explain that there are three separate sounds in the word **bat**. Take away the Sound Cards. Say the word **bat**, and tap out the three separate sounds without the cards. Tell the student to try to picture the three cards in his mind, even though they are no longer on the table. Say /**b**/, /**a**/, /**t**/, and tap thumb to finger for each sound. Now re-tap with fingers but this time say letter name rather than the sound. Repeat this procedure with other appropriate spelling words. Then dictate a word without first getting the corresponding cards. Tap out sounds and have student repeat. Then find the corresponding cards and place them together to form the word. Next, dictate a word and have the student try tapping out the sounds and find the corresponding cards. Have him tap out sounds and then name the corresponding letters. Dictate several words, including words with digraphs such as **shop**. These words will also get three taps: /**sh**/ - /**o**/ - /**p**/.

Initially, avoid **ck** words. When the student is ready, make the word **duck** with Sound Cards. Ask the student "What says /**k**/?" (**c**, **k**, **ck**). Have the student find the **c** and **k** cards. Cover the **ck** with the **c** and then the **k**, then go back to **ck**.

As you do this, explain that at the **end** of the word (after the short vowel), the **ck** should be used. Practice with additional **ck** words.

PART 8   **PART 9**   **PART 10**   Follow the procedures for 8, 9, and 10.

Helpful Hints / Activities

Use cardboard to make a tachistoscope. Make strips of words to target "trouble spots" such as **b** and **p**. You can also make a wheel to practice trouble spots.

To Practice Vowels for Spelling (Lesson Plan Part 7)

Use a large index card for each vowel. Write the letter and make a long line followed by a picture of the keyword:

Model 'reading' the card: /ă/..........**pple**. Extend the /ă/ sound while you trace the line and finish the word when you get to the picture. When the student correctly does this activity, dictate a word and have the student repeat the word and tap it out. Next, have him tap again, stopping at the vowel and extending the vowel sound. The cards can be used to see which keyword can be finished after extending the sound. For example, dictate the word **lap**. The student taps, stops at the /ă/ sound, extends it and locates the card that allows him to slide his finger into the word /ă/..........**pple**. The extended sound /ă/ will not finish any other keyword.

Notes / FYI

If the student knows real words by sight, spend time to master these sounds using the nonsense wordlists. It is very important that the student gains an understanding of reading and spelling by sounds. Do not allow guessing. The student must become proficient at giving the sounds when presented with the Sound Cards. He must also become proficient at naming the correct letter or letters when asked, "What says __?" Blending and segmentation skills must be developed here. Do not progress until students can independently blend and segment the sounds in a word.

When forming real and nonsense words with Sound Cards, avoid using **r**, **h**, **w**, **y** and **wh** at the end. Make short vowel words only!

1.4 What to Teach

- **ll**, **ss**, **ff** spelling rule

- **a** sound when followed by **ll** (**all**)

Additional Materials Needed
- Green **all** Sound Card

- 1.4 Word Cards

PART 1

For the first lesson in Step 1.4, no new sound is added to the quick drill. In subsequent lessons, include the green **all** card in the quick drill.

PART 2

Have student read **mis** with cards on table. Tell the student that this has three sounds but it needs another **s**. Add the other **s** card to make the word **miss**. Even though there are two **s**'s, there is only one sound. Tap out **miss** (three taps). This happens when an **s** follows a short vowel to end the word. Demonstrate with other words such as **lass**, **kiss**, **fuss**, etc. Repeat the same with double **l** (**ll**) and double **f** (**ff**) words (**bill**, **tell**, **buff**, etc.).

Teach **all** immediately or wait until subsequent lessons, depending upon student's ability.

Tell students that **all** changes the short **a** sound to /ȯ/. Teach this sound using the green **all** Sound Card. Add this card to students known sound pack. Make **all** words with the cards on the table: b all

Green cards in the Wilson program are "welded" sounds. Younger students can call them "glued" sounds. The **all**, for example, is not **one** sound, it is two (/ȯ/ and /l/). The second **l** is silent. First tap out /ȯ/, /l/, /l/, using index finger then middle finger. Any sounds on green cards, however, get "welded" together. Thus, to tap out /ȯ/, /l/, weld two fingers together and tap them to the thumb at the same time /ȯl/. To tap out **ball**: /b/ gets tapped with one finger and /ȯl/ gets one tap with two fingers at the same time. If a student is unable to do this, they can simply tap /b/, /ȯl/: **b** with one finger, /ȯl/ with one finger.

Notebook Entry
(Spelling Rules Section) The student should enter the first spelling rule into his or her notebook in the section for spelling. Read the rule to the student. Explain it again and have the student write examples.

PART 3   **PART 4**   **PART 5**

Follow the procedures for Parts 3, 4, and 5.

PART 6

Spread out Sound Cards (see Substep 1.3) Be sure to include green **all** card with other cards when you spread out the cards for sound dictation. Dictate "What says /ȯl/?" (**all**), as well as review sounds.

PART 7 Include the extra **l**, **s** and **f** cards when you spread out the cards. Dictate the word **fill**. Have the student repeat the word and tap it out /**f**/ - /**ĭ**/ - /**l**/. It gets only three taps since it has three sounds. The student should then find the corresponding letters **fil** and add the other **l** card for the bonus letter. Lastly, the student must orally spell the word. Practice 1.4 words, then mix 1.3 and 1.4 words. Students add the bonus letter card as needed.

After the **all** sound is taught, dictate **all** words. The student taps the word and finds the cards. The green **all** card should be used for the /**ȯl**/ sound.

PART 8 **PART 9** **PART 10** Follow the procedures for Parts 8, 9, and 10.

Helpful Hints / Activities

Tell the student that **l**, **s** and **f** are bonus letters. After a short vowel these letters get a bonus. Make a sheet of words and tell students to add the bonus letter when needed. Examples:

bel	**tax**
pat	**fus**
muf	**tin**
lad	**mil**

To reinforce this, have students star (*) bonus letters in a wordlist.

miss*

Notes / FYI

If a word has one **l**, the vowel is short, as expected (**pal**, **gal**, **Sal**, **Cal**).

There are a few words that don't get a bonus letter (**bus**, **yes**). Do not call these exceptions. Only use the word "exception" when referring to the exception to each syllable type. For each syllable type, students will learn an exception. Words such as **yes**, **bus**, etc. are words that the student may already know. If not, the word can be put into the Sight Word Dictionary in the Student's Notebook to be memorized.

Words with /**z**/ sound of **s** are never doubled. These are taught as sight words (**has**, **is**, etc.).

Some words ending in **z** also double after a short vowel (**fuzz**, **buzz**, **jazz**).

"Tapping" always represents the **sounds** in a given word. Therefore, when tapping the green cards, be sure fingers used represent the sounds. **All** - tap with two fingers welded since it is two sounds (not three). The word **mall** has a total of **three** sounds: **m** - one, **all** - two. If this confuses the student, it is okay to tap /**ȯl**/ with only one finger. **However, the teacher should understand that /ȯl/ is not one sound or three sounds, but two**. The question to the student, "How many sounds in that word?" should be avoided with /**ȯl**/ since it is confusing.

Weave with Questions

"What are the bonus letters?"
"Is there a bonus letter in that word or sentence?"
"Put a star above any bonus letter."

1.5   What to Teach

· **am** and **an** "welded" sounds

Additional Materials Needed
· Green **am** and **an** cards   · 1.5 Word Cards

PART 1
Have the student make the sound /**m**/. While making the sound, have him block his nose. The sound cannot be made with the nose blocked. Do the same with /**n**/. **M** and **n** are called nasal sounds because the sound comes out of the nose. Due to this quality, **m** and **n** sometimes distort a vowel sound, especially **a**. Produce the **am** and **an** green cards. Explain that these are welded sounds. The **n** and **m** change the short **a** sound from a pure short **a** to a nasal sound. The **a** is still considered short. Most students have no difficulty with this. It is especially important for sound segmentation (tapping). It is much easier to read and spell these words when **an** and **am** are welded rather than segmented (**p - an**, not **p - a - n**).

Notebook Entry
(Sound Section) Add **am** and **an** beside short **a** on the short vowel sound page.

PART 2
Use **b** and **a** Sound Cards. Add a consonant at the end to make words, including **bat**, **back** and **bad**. Now put **m** at the end. Explain again that **m** changes the sound of **a**. Replace the **a m** with the green **am** card. Demonstrate tapping /**b**/ - **b** - one tap, /**am**/ - two fingers welded, tapped together. Do words with **pa** such as **pat**, **pad** and **pal**. Now make **p a n**. Change the **a n** cards to the green **an** card. Make **am** and **an** words using the Sound Cards. Have the student tap and read these words.

PART 3 **PART 4** **PART 5**

Follow the procedures for Parts 3, 4, and 5.

PART 6
Be sure to ask "What says /**am**/?" and "What says /**an**/?"

PART 7
Dictate **am** and **an** words. Be sure student taps out sounds: /**p**/ - one tap, /**an**/ - two fingers welded together in one tap. The **p** ivory card and **an** green card should be selected. Be sure the student orally spells the word after tapping and finding cards. This can be done while tapping yet again: **p - an**.

PART 8 **PART 9** **PART 10**

Follow the procedures for Parts 8, 9, and 10.

Notes / FYI
am, **an** - tap with 2 fingers welded since it is two sounds. The word **man** has **3** sounds: **m** = 1, **an** = 2.

Weave with Questions
"Where is the **a** nasal sound?" Box welded sounds **p** [**an**]

1.6   What to Teach

- Concept of baseword and suffix
- /**z**/ sound of **s**
- How to read and spell 3-sound words with suffix -**s** added

Additional Materials Needed
- 1.6 Word Cards

 PART 1 For the first lesson in 1.6, no new sound is added to the quick drill. In subsequent lessons, the student should give both sounds of **s** when presented with the **s** card: **s** - **snake** - /**s**/, **s** - **bugs** - /**z**/.

 PART 2 Begin this Substep by making the word **shop** with Sound Cards. Have the student read it. Add the **s** card to form the word **shops**. Tell the student that **shop** is the baseword and the suffix -**s** can be added to it.

Do the same thing with **bug**. Read the word **bug**, using Sound Cards. Add **s** to form **bugs**. Explain that the **s** sounds like a /**z**/ sometimes when added to words as a suffix.

When reading these words in isolation, the student must always say the baseword, then the whole word (**shop**, **shops** - **bug**, **bugs**). This is first taught with the Sound Cards, then applied to Word Cards and wordlist reading. This habit helps focus their attention on the structure of the word. Only the baseword is tapped out - the suffix isn't tapped. Students tap the baseword only if they have difficulty decoding.

Notebook Entry
(Sound Section) The sound of /**z**/ for **s**, as in **bugs** is entered in the sound section.

(Spelling Section) The definition of baseword and suffix is added to the student's notebook. Begin the list with **s** suffix.

 PART 3   **PART 4**   **PART 5**   Follow the procedures for Parts 3, 4, and 5.

 PART 6 Include "What says /**z**/?" Now, both **z** and **s** should be the response.

 PART 7 For spelling, the student must name and spell the baseword first, and then add the **s**. Spread out the Sound Cards. Make the word **bugs**. Ask the students to read the word, including the suffix (**bugs**). Remove the suffix -**s** and ask, "What is the baseword?" (**bug**). Make another word with the suffix -**s**, have the student read it, remove the **s** and name the baseword. Next, do this orally, without the cards. You say a word such as **pens**. The student should repeat (**pens**) then name the (**pen**). When the student is able to do this, dictate a 1.6 word such as **rugs**.

The student should repeat the word (**rugs**), name the baseword (**rug**) and then find the letters (**r u g**).

If needed, the student can tap out the baseword. If the baseword is correctly spelled, the student adds the suffix -**s**. Dictate several words to practice.

PART 8   PART 9   PART 10   Follow the procedures for Parts 8, 9, and 10.

Notes / FYI
In some words the sound of the final consonant may "get lost" when the suffix -**s** is added. For example, it is difficult to hear the **t** in the word **nets**. The student **must** name and spell **net** and then add **s**.

Weave with Questions
"What is the baseword?"

"What it the suffix?"

Underline basewords, circle suffix -**s**:

<u>bug</u>(s)

Optional
On wordlists, mark above the **s** with an /**s**/ or /**z**/ to indicate the sound.

Step 2

At the end of this step, students should know:

- The welded sounds: **ing**, **ang**, **ong**, **ung**, **ink**, **ank**, **onk**, **unk**
- The definition of a syllable
- How to identify a closed syllable
- The difference between a blend and a digraph
- How to blend sounds and read words or nonsense syllables with a short vowel (up to six sounds)
- How to segment sounds and spell words with a short vowel (up to six sounds)
- How to read and spell **ild**, **old**, **olt**, **ost** and **ind** words

In Step 2, you will continue to work with short vowels. The student will learn how to blend and segment four sounds, then five sounds, then six sounds in a given syllable. Students must be able to segment the sounds independently. If a student cannot do this, do not move on, even if the student reads and spells the words correctly. This mastery is essential for future success. You will use Sound Cards, blank cards, and finger tapping to teach this skill. Use nonsense syllables as well as real words.

At the beginning of this step, the student will learn about closed syllables. Emphasize this concept throughout the step. It is important that the student visually recognizes closed syllables. The student should know that **if** a syllable is closed **then** the vowel sound is short.

2.1 What to Teach

- New "welded" sounds: **ang**, **ing**, **ong**, **ung**, **ank**, **ink**, **onk**, and **unk**
- How to read and spell words with the above sounds
- Definition of a syllable
- How to identify a closed syllable

Additional Materials Needed

- Green Sound Cards for the welded sounds listed above
- 2.1 Word Cards
- Step 2 Student Reader and Student Rules Notebook
- Student Workbook 2A & 2B (optional)
- Supplemental readings for B Level students: Travels with Ted, Stories for Students 1-2-3
- It is usually best to divide this Substep into two parts rather than teach it all at once:

    1 the introduction of **ing** / **ink** sounds

    2 the introduction of closed syllable concept

PART 1

Students must learn the following letter combinations:

ang - fang	ing - ring	ong - song	ung - lung
ank - bank	ink - pink	onk - honk	unk - junk

Present these sounds with green Sound Cards and keywords. Explain that the three letters do have individual sounds, but that the sounds are very closely welded together and are therefore difficult to separate. To tap this out, use three fingers tapping together - at the same time. Tap on table rather than to thumb if this is easier for the student. Explain that the three fingers represent the three individual sounds (see Notes / FYI). These are said almost at the same time so it is easier to 'weld' them together. For example, **sink** would be tapped: **s** (one tap)   **ink** (one tap with three fingers)

Notebook Entry

(Sound Section) The eight new welded sounds are found in the Rules Notebook and should be entered into the student's Sound Section.

PART 2

Display Cards

ang	ank
ing	ink
ong	onk
ung	unk

Read them: **/ang/**, **/ing/**, **/ong/**, **/ung/**, **/ank/**, **/ink/**, **/onk/**, **/unk/**. Then read them **/ang/**, **/ank/**, **/ing/**, **/ink/**, etc. Have the student practice after you. Now, place the **b** consonant card in front of **ang**. Tap out the word **bang**: **/b/** (one tap) - **/ang/** (one tap with three fingers). Create words with all of the welded sounds. Have the student tap and blend each word.

After these sound combinations are mastered, in subsequent lessons, teach about closed syllables. Explain that words have parts that go together called syllables. A syllable is a part of a word that can be pushed out in one breath. **Cat** is one syllable. **Catnip** has two syllables. There are six kinds of syllables. All the words so far have been closed syllables. Form the word **bat.** Tell the student that a closed syllable has one vowel only (point to **a**) and must be closed in (move the **t** closer to the **a** to show how it closes it in). A closed syllable gives the vowel the short sound; /ă/ is the short sound of **a.** Now remove the **b** to leave the word **at.** Tell the student that there need not be a consonant in front of the vowel. The important point is that one vowel (point to **a** and stress *one*) is closed in (move **t**) by at least *one* consonant. Make the word **bath.** Tell the student that it can be closed in with more than one consonant (point to **th**). Use the Sound Cards to form the following words:

Ask the student to point to the closed syllables (**such**, **it**). Discuss each word, asking the student to explain why or why not it is a closed syllable.

such has one vowel closed in with **ch**
she has one vowel but it is not closed in
it has one vowel closed in by **t**, no need for any letter before the vowel
loaf has two vowels (OK for demo but use **oa** card when in Step 9!)

The Sound Cards must be used to teach the closed syllable concept in a multisensory way. Use the procedure described to continually review this concept. Avoid using **h, r, y** and **w** at the end - **ah, bar, bay, saw**... these are not closed syllables. Do not explain them yet, just avoid them! Teach the student how to 'mark' a closed syllable:

<u>s ŭ c h</u>
   c

Notebook Entry
(Syllable Section) Students must begin the syllable section of their notebook. Use the Rules Notebook to copy the definition of a syllable, and the closed syllable description and examples.

PART 3
Follow the procedure for Part 3.

PART 4
The words in 2.1 are limited. The A and B vocabulary is mixed together. Note that at the end of the Substep there is a page of words with suffix **-s.** Be sure to practice these in Parts 2 and 3 before presenting this list to students (see Notes / FYI).

PART 5
Follow the procedure for Part 5.

PART 6
Spread out new welded sounds as well as previous sounds. Ask "What Says ___?" including new sounds.

PART 7
Dictate one word from a pair such as **wing** - **wink** or **rang** - **rank.** Have student tap out the word then identify correct welded sound by pointing to the green Sound Card and naming the letters.

Spread new Sound Cards on the table along with several consonant and digraph Sound Cards already learned (**b**, **s**, **w**, **th**, etc.). Dictate a 2.1 word (such as **wink**) and ask the student to tap out the word and then to select the cards needed to form the word. Use the green card for spelling welded sounds rather than the peach vowel card followed by two consonant cards. Be sure the student orally spells the word after finding the letters.

 PART 8 **PART 9** **PART 10**   Follow the procedures for Parts 8, 9, and 10.

 Notes / FYI

Technically **ng** is a digraph and **nk** is a blend. Students learn these sounds best, however, when presented with a vowel sound. Thus, teach them as 'welded'. The discussion of blend versus digraph should be avoided unless questioned by student.

Be sure to emphasize that a closed syllable is a syllable that has one vowel, not a short vowel. The fact that it is closed **tells** the student the vowel is short. This is important because the teaching of the syllable type is to aid in the decoding of unknown words. If the student doesn't know a word (such as **vat**), he can figure it out by determining if it is a closed syllable, then applying the short sound (using the keyword **apple**). The goal is to teach the student to **recognize** when a syllable is closed by seeing the pattern. When a student is asked to describe a closed syllable, don't have him say, "a closed syllable is a syllable with a short vowel." Rather, the response should be, "a closed syllable is a syllable with one vowel, closed in by consonant(s) and this **tells** us the vowel is short." The purpose of teaching this is so that the student knows **how** to read the vowel.

Reminder

Words with a suffix: for both reading and spelling, student **taps only the baseword**, not the suffix -**s**.

Reading
Words in isolation are read:

Word	How it is read
chills	**chill** - **chills**
winks	**wink** - **winks**

Spelling

Teacher Dictates:	Student repeats the word, then names the baseword
songs	**songs** - **song**
	The student spells **s o n g** and then adds **s**.

 Weave with Questions

Box any welded sounds **s** $\boxed{\text{ing}}$

"Is this word a closed syllable?" If yes, "What does that tell you about the vowel?" or "Find closed syllables in this sentence and 'mark' them." <u>c ă t</u>
c

2.2   What to Teach

· The difference between a blend and a digraph

· How to identify and read a blend and segment up to four sounds in a closed syllable

Additional Materials Needed
· 2.2 Word Cards

PART 1   Follow the procedure for Part 1.

PART 2   Students must learn the definition of a blend. Review the closed syllable concept, using Sound Cards. Then, review the concept of a digraph. Spread out the digraph Sound Cards (**ch**, **sh**, **ck**, **th**, **wh**). Re-explain how a digraph contains two consonants, yet it makes only one sound. Let the student give the sound for each digraph.

Using Sound Cards, form the word **ship**. The student must read the word and identify the digraph. Now, form the word **slip**. Explain that this word is also formed by two consonants, a vowel and another consonant. There is, however, a big difference between the word **ship** and **slip**. Tap out **ship** (3 taps). Tap out **slip** by tapping one finger over each card in the word. Explain that **slip** has four sounds because **s** and **l** each have their own sound. That is why **s** and **l** have their own cards - unlike the **sh** card. Tell the student that when there are two or more consonants together, each making their own sound, it is called a blend. These sounds can be pulled apart (pull **s** and **l** cards apart) **s l i p**, but the two consonants blend together nicely. Separate **s** and **l** Sound Cards, then push them together as student practices saying sounds individually and then, blended. Follow this example with several other 2.2 words. Pull blends apart (separating Sound Cards) while student says each individual sound. Put blends together (joining Sound Cards), as student reads letters to blend them together. Show students that blends may appear before a vowel (**brag**) or after a vowel (**sent**). Both are closed syllables since they have one vowel, closed in by at least one consonant. Have the student tap out sounds and read the words.

Demonstrate a digraph blend with Sound Cards (**nch** in **lunch**, **shr** in **shred**). These words also have four sounds. A digraph is blended with another consonant. Call this a digraph blend.

After the student masters blending four sounds, use Sound Cards to review the reading of a baseword + suffix. Make the word **drum** and add the suffix -**s**. These words should be read: **drum** - **drums**.

Notebook Entry
(Sound Section) Enter the definition of a blend.

PART 3   Follow the procedure for Part 3.

PART 4   The student should read wordlists with 4-sound words and when mastered, read these words with the suffix -**s** added. A wordlist in the Student Reader provides this practice. The students should tap out the baseword only (as needed). These words should be read: **drop** - **drops**, **loft** - **lofts**.

Follow the procedures for Parts 5 and 6.

 For Spelling, students must now learn to "pull apart" 4 sounds. Do this with cards, tapping above each sound (**s t e p**). Then take away cards and say the same word (**step**). Instruct students to tap sounds, visualizing cards in their minds. Repeat this with several 2.2 words.

Spread out the Sound Cards and dictate a 2.2 word. Have student repeat the word and tap it out. Ask the student to try to picture the cards in his mind as he says each sound separately. The student should then find the cards to correspond with each tap.

The blank phoneme cards can also be used rather than the actual letter cards. The student "spells" the word with the correct color blank cards to represent sounds in the word dictated. Actually, it is essential that the student can use blank cards to spell any Step 1 or Step 2 word before moving onto Step 3, so begin this process now. The correct representation of a word with blank cards shows that the student has internalized the phoneme segmentation skills that are critical for success beyond Step 2.

When the student masters the segmentation and spelling of words with four sounds, dictate words with four sounds and the suffix, -**s**. You say the word (**drums**). The student repeats the word, names the **baseword**, taps the baseword, and finds the corresponding letters. The suffix -**s** is then added.

   Follow the procedures for Parts 8, 9, and 10.

 Notes / FYI

Words that have nasal **a** /**am**/ and /**an**/ embedded in the word can be difficult. Example words: **lamp** or **land**. It works best to use the green **am** and **an** cards to read and spell these words. Be aware of these sounds within words so that you can target it as a trouble spot as needed. The **mp** in **lamp** and **nd** in **land** are blends.

It is essential to frequently review closed syllable concept in this Substep. This needs to be solid in order to teach the exceptions in Substep 2.3.

Common spelling errors include the omission of **l**, **r**, **n**, **m** from consonant blends. Blends with these consonants may need additional practice. End blends with **l**, **n** and **m** can be particularly troublesome.

Discuss the terms blend, digraph, and closed syllable throughout this Substep.

 Weave with Questions

"Where is the blend?" or "Where is the digraph blend?"
Continue asking, "Is this a closed syllable?"
"How many sounds in that word?" (Avoid this question when the word contains a **ng** or **nk** welded sound.)

Have the student underline blends after spelling words on paper (<u>s</u> tash). Use two lines to indicate two separate sounds.

2.3   What to Teach

· New welded sounds: **ind**, **ild**, **old**, **olt**, **ost**

· Exception to closed syllable

Additional Materials Needed

· Green Sound Cards: **ind**, **ild**, **old**, **olt**, **ost**

· 2.3 Word Cards

In the Wilson Reading System, the word "exception" is only used for the exception to syllable types. Otherwise, the student gets frustrated with so many exceptions.

Be sure the student has thoroughly mastered the concept of closed syllable. They should visually recognize these and be able to give the vowel sound.

PART 1

Teach the student that there are five exceptions to the closed syllable rule. Ask what kind of sound the vowel has in a closed syllable (short). For example, in the word **past**, the **a** is closed in by a consonant. This gives **a** the /ă/ sound, as in **apple**. Use the green cards (**ind**, **ild**, **old**, **olt**, **ost**) to show students that whenever these letters are in a closed syllable, the vowel usually says its own name, rather than the short sound. Explain that this is the long sound of the vowel.

Students say "**o l d** - **cold** - /**old**/" when the green card is presented during the quick drill.

Point out that three of these begin with **o** and two begin with **i**. Two have **ld** following the vowel. Students need to know these to mastery so that when asked, "What are the exceptions to the closed syllable?" they can answer: **ind**, **ild**, **old**, **olt**, **ost**.

Notebook Entry

(Syllable Section) Use the Rules Notebook to copy the exceptions to the closed syllable in the Syllable Section.

PART 2

Use the Sound Cards to make the word **cold**. Demonstrate how to tap this: /**c**/ - one tap (index finger to thumb) and /**old**/ - one tap (three fingers welded). Have the student practice reading words with the closed syllable exceptions, using the green exception cards. Have him tap as needed.

Show the word **wind** (short vowel) with **w**, **i** (peach card), **n** and **d** (ivory cards) and **wind** (long vowel) with **w** and **ind** (green card). **Wind** (short) is **not** an exception to the exception. Rather, this **follows** the closed syllable rule. This is also true of **cost**, **lost** and any others that have a short sound.

Initially, it helps to keep the exception green cards spread out for reference throughout lesson.

PART 3   **PART 4**   **PART 5**

Follow the procedures for Parts 3, 4, and 5.

PART 6 Spread out Sound Cards, including new green cards with the exceptions. Include the dictation of the exception sounds: "What Says /**ind**/?" etc.

PART 7 Use green exception cards (**ild**, **old**, **olt**, **ind**, **ost**). Also, spread out some consonant Sound Cards or blank ivory cards. Dictate a 2.3 word such as **find**. The student must tap out the word /**f**/ - /**ind**/, and select the corresponding cards. The student then must re-tap while orally spelling the word.

PART 8 **PART 9** **PART 10** Follow the procedures for Parts 8, 9, and 10.

Weave with Questions

"Find the exceptions to the closed syllable"

"Is the vowel long or short?"

Teach students how to mark words with exceptions:

$$c\,h\,\bar{i}\,l\,d$$

"What do vowels say in closed syllables?"

"Name the exceptions to the closed syllable rule."

2.4 What to Teach

· How to blend and segment up to five sounds in a closed syllable

Additional Materials Needed
· 2.4 Word Cards

PART 1

Follow the procedure for Part 1.

PART 2

Some words have five sounds in a syllable. Make the word **skunk** with cards. This word has five sounds, even though the **unk** gets welded together. Practice tapping and reading words with five sounds including a welded sound. Next, place Sound Cards on the table to form the word **lump**. The student must tap out the sounds. Ask him, "How many sounds are in this word?" Add **c** to make **clump**. Point out that it now has five sounds, with a blend before the vowel (**cl**), and a blend after the vowel (**mp**). To tap words with five sounds, reuse the index finger or tap on the table using the thumb for first tap.

In some words, a digraph will combine with a consonant to form a digraph blend. Use cards on the table to demonstrate **shrimp**: sh r i m p Tap and count the sounds.

PART 3

Follow the procedure for Part 3.

PART 4

Be aware of the wordlist choices. Some lists contain words with welded sounds such as **blink** whereas other lists have two blends such as **clump**. Be sure to do both kinds of words before moving to 2.5. Also, do words with the suffix -**s**.

PART 5 **PART 6**

Follow the procedures for Parts 5 and 6.

PART 7

The first words in 2.4 have welded sounds; though they have five sounds (**flunk**) they are easier than the words with two blends (**clump**). The green welded Sound Cards should be used to spell these words. Also, use the blank cards: ivory - ivory - green for the word **flunk**. The student must then name the letter(s) that correspond with each blank card.

Next, spread out Sound Cards. Dictate a 4-sound word and have student select cards to form the word. Then name a 5-sound word that requires one additional sound. Have the student add the appropriate card to form the 5-sound word. Words to use for this activity include:

stun - stunt	runt - grunt	lump - clump
lend - blend	last - blast	lint - flint
raft - draft	slum - slump	tram - tramp

Next, the student must learn to tap each sound separately. Dictate a 2.4 word such as **stunt**. The student must repeat the word, then tap out the individual sounds. Tell the student to be sure he taps out five sounds. (If he taps **st u n t**, show him with the Sound Cards that **s** and **t** each make a separate sound. Put the word out with cards and tap over it.) After tapping the sounds, the student should find the letters that correspond with each tap, then spell orally. Blank cards can also be used: ivory - ivory - peach - ivory - ivory. The student then must name the letters to go on each blank card. Dictate several words to the student for practice.

PART 8   PART 9   PART 10   Follow the procedures for Parts 8, 9, and 10.

Notes / FYI

Be sure to follow the procedure for reading and spelling words with suffix -**s** when these Substep words are presented to students.

Weave with Questions

Ask "Where are the blends in this word?"

Ask "How many sounds in this word?" when a word has two blends such as **clump**. Avoid this question with the words with a welded sound because technically **ank** is a blend and **ng** is a digraph. Thus, **clang** has four sounds and **clank** has five sounds. This is confusing and need not be taught.

2.5   What to Teach

- · 3-letter blends

- · How to blend and segment up to six sounds in a closed syllable

Additional Materials Needed
- · 2.5 Word Cards

 PART 1   Follow the procedure for Part 1.

 PART 2   Use the Sound Cards to review the closed syllable concept, closed syllable exceptions, and the difference between a digraph and a blend. Make the word **trap** with cards. Have the student read it and
identify the blend. Ask how many sounds in the blend (two). Now add the **s** card to form the word
strap. Point out the **str** blend and explain that three consonants might be together, each making a
separate sound. This is called a 3-letter blend. Each letter in a blend makes a sound, thus each gets a
tap. Count the sounds in **strap** (five). Make additional 2.5 words. Show the students that some of these
words have six sounds such as **script**. Words with six sounds have a 3-letter blend and a 2-letter blend.
These words can be segmented into six sounds.

 PART 3   Review by spreading out Word Cards 2.1 - 2.5. Ask questions such as: "Find and read all words with
closed syllable exceptions,...3-letter blends...that start with a digraph and end with a blend", etc.

 PART 4   **PART 5**   **PART 6**   Follow the procedures for Parts 4, 5, and 6.

 PART 7   Put together three blank ivory cards, a peach card and then another ivory card. Dictate the word **strap**.
Have the student repeat the word and then find the corresponding Sound Cards to put on top of the
blank cards to spell the word. The student should then orally spell the word. After doing several 2.5
words in this manner, rather than providing the student with the blank cards, dictate a word and have
him repeat the word, tap it, and select the blank cards needed. Then, pointing to the blank cards, the
student should spell the word.

string - ivory, ivory, ivory, green   **splash** - ivory, ivory, ivory, peach, ivory etc.

 PART 8   **PART 9**   **PART 10**   Follow the procedures for Parts 8, 9, and 10.

 Weave with Questions
"Is there a 3-letter blend in this word?"
"What letters are in the blend?"
"How many sounds are in this word?" Again, avoid this question with words containing welded
sounds.

Step 3

At the end of this step, students should know:

- That syllables can be combined to make longer words
- How to divide two- and three-syllable words
- How to read/spell two- and three-syllable words that combine closed syllables
- The spelling of **ct** and **ic** within words

Step 3 begins work with multi-syllables. Students will learn how to segment syllables just as they segmented sounds. They no longer tap sounds to read unless they have difficulty. In order to move into Step 3, it is essential that the student can **fluently** blend (without tapping) any nonsense Step 1 and Step 2 syllables. Also, the student must be able to independently segment the sound in words with up to six sounds. This is necessary for success in Step 3.

Students will work with words combining two **closed** syllables. After dividing the word into syllables, the students should easily read each syllable, then put it altogether. If a student has trouble with one of the 'parts' then that syllable may be tapped out. If a student consistently cannot read a part without tapping, you moved too quickly through Steps 1 and 2.

There are no new sounds taught in Step 3. The student will learn about schwa, as it applies to the vowel sound in unaccented syllables.

Syllable Division

Syllable division is taught throughout Step 3. Syllable Cards can be used in Parts 2 and 7 of the lesson. The **Sound Cards** must be used to initially demonstrate syllable division and other concepts, but it then becomes cumbersome to use Sound Cards and subsequent words can be demonstrated with the Syllable Cards. Students underline or 'scoop' syllables rather than slash them:

<u>cat</u> <u>nip</u>   or   **catnip**   not   **cat/nip**

The slash can be visually confusing. The most important reason however is to encourage the syllable division of words while reading them left to right. Underlining is done from left to right. Students should divide words to read them throughout this step. We **do not** mark words with a more complicated type of system: c v c c v c
p u b l i c

Don't do it that way! Reasons: It is more than is necessary. It doesn't help students to quickly divide a word as they move their eyes across the word. It takes away from the word to focus on identifying vowels and consonants. Lastly, it is less efficient than having students learn to scan for digraphs, etc. You will find that syllable division is easily taught if Step 2 was thoroughly taught and the **Sound Cards** are used to master the principles. Syllable division will also be taught in a step-by-step manner, thus not overwhelming the student with too many principles at once. Initially, the "rules" applicable to closed syllables are the only ones the student needs to apply.

Students should always read with a pencil or pen point in hand so that the point can be used to divide words and track as needed. An unleaded pencil or retracted ball point pen can be used so that the student doesn't imprint the page in the book.

3.1   What to Teach

· Combining two closed syllables (up to three sounds per syllable) into multisyllabic words

· Syllable division principles

· The spelling of words by syllable (one syllable at a time)

Advanced Students

· Unexpected vowel sounds due to accent (schwa)

· **e** = /**i**/ in some closed syllables

Additional Materials Needed

· Schwa Sound Card (this will not be needed initially)

· 3.1 Syllable Cards, 3.1 Word Cards

· Step 3 Student Reader and Student Rules Notebook

· Student Workbook 3A (optional)

This Substep begins one of the most important concepts in the program; sounds are built into syllables and syllables are combined to form words. The student must **see and hear** words in parts. This is often very exciting for the students and, of course, very rewarding for the teacher. Read through this Substep carefully. Practice teaching this Substep. Do not allow the student to look at the whole word and guess while reading. If a word is unknown, the student(s) must learn to divide the word and decode it one syllable at a time. Likewise for spelling: students must learn to spell one syllable at a time for success. This will take "training." This Substep contains various types of words. As you will see, they vary due to syllable division rules, and vowel sounds due to accent. For this reason, be sure to carefully select wordlists and be thorough. Do not rush this Substep.

Initially, skip Part 1, 6 and 7 teaching of schwa. Wait to read about it until you are ready to teach it so that you can concentrate on the other concepts. The explanation of schwa is described at the end of this Substep.

PART 1

No new sounds are taught, so review learned sounds and move to Part 2. After several lessons, when the student has mastered the syllable division principles, the schwa vowel variant can be introduced (see the instructions at the end of this Substep).

PART 2

Tell the student that words are made up of parts. Sounds go together to make each part. Sometimes there is only one part and other times, more than one. The word **cat** has one part made up of three sounds. The word **catnip** has two parts. You can hear it. Each part is one push of breath. When another push of breath is needed it is a new part. Give the student words orally. The student should listen and name the number of parts. Now tell the student that to read or spell longer words, he just has to do one part at a time. Tell him that he can already read the part separately, so it will be easy to read and spell longer words – one part at a time. Put **b a th** on the table or magnetic board and let the student read it. Next, put **t u b** out, and have him read this part. Now combine the parts to form **bathtub**. Read each part; then read it together. Scoop your finger under each part as it is read. Explain that each part is one push of breath. Tell the student that the words in Step 3 combine closed syllables to form longer words.

To begin this Substep, use both Sound Cards and Syllable Cards to demonstrate various 3.1 words, dividing the words for the student. Then make the word **napkin** with the Sound Cards but do not split it into two syllables. Point out that the two vowels in this word are separated by consonants. This is easy to see with the different color cards used to represent vowels and consonants. The peach vowel cards are not together. Tell the student that whenever vowels are separated, the word must be split into two parts or syllables somewhere between the two separated vowels.

There are three 'rules' of syllable division taught in 3.1. These must be taught and practiced with **Sound** Cards initially. After teaching each of the following principles with the Sound Cards, make other examples and ask the student the following:

"Should we divide this word? Why?" (two vowels are separated)

"Where would you divide?" Then have them separate the Sound Cards to make two syllables.

1   Divide between two consonants. Demonstrate this with example words such as **sunfish**, **catnip**, **cactus** and **tennis**. To make a word such as **tennis**, simply use a blank white index card to make an extra **n** card.

2   For now, when there is only one consonant, that consonant is needed to close in the first syllable. Demonstrate this with examples such as **habit** and **relish**. In the word **relish**, the **l** must go with the first syllable in order to make it a closed syllable. Since Step 3 only has closed syllables, both the first and the second syllable must be closed.

3   With three consonants between two vowels, including a digraph, the digraph stays together. Also, if there is only a digraph between the two vowels, keep it together to close in the first syllable. Show examples such as **bathtub**, **nutshell** and **rocket**.

Notebook Entry
(Syllable Section) Add Syllable Division Rules for 3.1. On the closed syllable page, add "Closed syllables can be combined..."

(Spelling Section) Add 3.1 reason to double consonants.

PART 3   Add 3.1 Word Cards. Continue to review words from other Substeps. If needed initially, make Word
     Cards with two syllables written in two different colors to aid student.

Suggested Activities
Students should make a personal set of Word Cards so the teacher set is not used. Students can scoop words into two syllables on Word Cards.

Students can classify words into groups depending upon syllable division principle applied (see three principles for groupings).

PART 4 Use Student Reader 3 and select an A or B list as appropriate. Be sure to identify the **type** of list you want the student to practice and chart. You will be able to determine the type of words on the list by the sample word provided in the upper right-hand corner of the list. Be sure that similar words were introduced and practiced in Parts 2 and 3. Examples:

sunfish = compound word
cactus = split between 2 consonants
relish = divide after consonant
rocket = digraph stays together
ə = schwa words
e says /ĭ/ = **e** says /ĭ/

Compound words are the easiest words in Step 3. This is because the two short words might be easily recognized. Usually, the syllables in a compound word have equal stress (accent), so there tends not to be a schwa sound.

PART 5 Since words within context are easier to decode, the sentence pages do not categorize the words. Be aware of unaccented vowel sounds so that you can assist the student as needed.

skip **PART 6** Initially no new sounds are added. Continue to review. See the "What Says" page in the Dictation Book.

PART 7 The most important thing with multisyllabic spelling is the change in procedure. Now students segment **syllables** rather than sounds. They no longer tap out individual sounds unless they have difficulty. It is easiest to teach this with Syllable Cards to represent each syllable. Initially, have students simply learn to say a two-syllable word in two parts or two separate breaths. Be careful not to 'feed' the student one syllable at a time. You must dictate the entire word and the student must learn to segment it into its parts. Two blank index cards can be used and the students can simply repeat the dictated words while touching an index card to represent each syllable. When the students understand this, use the Syllable Cards to make the word **punish**. Turn the cards over so the blank side is face up.

| pun | ish | | |

Say the word, **punish** and have student(s) repeat.

- Student then says the word, dividing it into parts while pointing to blank Syllable Cards to represent the syllable parts.

- Student says the first syllable, spells first syllable, then turns the card over to check it. The student says the second syllable, spells the second syllable then turns the card over to check it.

- The student then **immediately** reads word back while scooping syllables from left to right with his index finger. This is a **proofreading** technique that will be applied when the student writes the words in Part 8.

The multisyllabic spelling procedure must be practiced with many examples using Syllable Cards. It is critical that the student learn to name and spell one syllable at a time. Avoid the Syllable Cards with the double consonants (see Notes / FYI).

The letters **l**, **s** and **f** do not double in multisyllabic words (**until**, **velvet**). The bonus letter rule applies to one-syllable words. Compound words with **ll**, **ss**, **ff** will remain doubled (**shellfish**, **bellman**).

When an **s** is added to a multisyllabic baseword, the student must spell the baseword, one syllable at a time and then add **s**. For example, **submits**: Student must say **submit** - **sub** (spell **s u b**), **mit** (spell **m i t**), then add the **s**.

Teach that multisyllabic words ending in **/ik/** are spelled **ic**, not **ik**. Some examples: **tonic**, **panic**. Use cards to practice these words.

Notebook Entry
(Spelling Section) Add **ic** to ways to spell /**k**/.

PART 8   Use Dictation Book to plan lesson.
Sounds: Dictate 5 sounds from the Dictation Book "What Says" page for Step 3.1.

Words: Multisyllabic Spelling Procedure: *this process will be followed for all multisyllabic words throughout the entire program*

1   Teacher says word, student repeats (**punish**)
2   Student says word in syllables while pointing to blank index cards to represent the syllable parts.
3   Student says first syllable, spells first syllable ("**pun   p** - **u** - **n**").
4   Student says second syllable, spells second syllable ("**ish   i** - **s** - **h**"). It is helpful to have student point to the blank index cards that represent the syllable being spelled.
5   The student then writes the word, naming each syllable and spelling it orally while writing it. Some students may need to orally spell and then write one syllable at a time. That is fine.
6   The student then immediately reads the word back while underlining syllables from left to right. This is done to teach the student to proofread. Be sure student looks carefully at the word when scooping the syllables: **p u n i s h**

Sentences: Dictate two or three sentences selected from 3.1 (A or B).

PART 9   **PART 10**   Follow the procedures for Parts 9, and 10.

Weave with Questions
Ask, "Should this word be divided? Where do you divide this word? Why?"
Students should scoop or underline syllables in words.

Helpful Hints / Activities
Write 3.1 words on large index cards. Make the vowels with a peach magic marker or crayon so they stand out. Have student(s) use scissors to cut cards into two syllables. Discuss syllable division principles as you do this activity.

Use WRS Syllable Cards. A match game can be used in Part 2 of the lesson. The student must read the first syllable and find its match.

vel	meg
nut	it
gob	vet
sub	mit
hab	lin

Notes / FYI

There are certain situations that do not usually present a problem for reading, especially when the vocabulary is known and the word is read within context. In an unaccented second syllable, when the letter **e** is followed by **t**, the **e** sounds like /ĭ/ (**velvet**). Also, in an unaccented second syllable, the consonants **t** or **d** followed by **en**: the vowel sound of **e** is "lost" (**mitten** = /mĭt n/). You should not necessarily teach these concepts to students. Most likely, they will have no problem decoding these words. Be aware of these factors when dictating the words for spelling. Discuss with student as needed.

Teaching Schwa

Schwa is not a phoneme, but a phonetic variant or reduced vowel. The schwa sound is most like the sound of short **u**, but not equal to it. Often, the second syllable in a two-syllable word is unaccented and the vowel sound is obscured. To teach the schwa sound for decoding, most students can simply be taught to try the schwa "sound" if the word doesn't seem right.

Advanced Students

PART 1

Take out the peach schwa card. Spread out all of the peach vowel cards, separating the **u** vowel card from the others. Teach the students that sometimes the vowels **a**, **e**, **i** and **o** sound more like the short **u** than the expected sound. **Proceed to the schwa section in Part 2**. In subsequent lessons, students can read the schwa card.

 (schwa) - **wagon** - /ŭ/

Notebook Entry

(Sound Section) Add schwa to the vowel page.

PART 2

Tell students that if a word is tricky to read and it doesn't sound right, they can try to use the /ŭ/ sound and see if it helps. Demonstrate with the word **wagon**. Show them how the **o** sounds more like /ŭ/. Cover the **o** vowel card with the schwa card. Tell them that when this happens it is called a schwa. Teach them to read the schwa card: ə (schwa) - **wagon** - /ŭ/

*Technically, schwa is not exactly the same sound of short **u** (/ŭ/). However, this association helps them to learn the obscure sound of schwa.*

Make additional words such as **lesson** and **salad**. Advanced students can be taught about accent and the details of the schwa sound (See: Notes / FYI). The schwa card should be added to the Part 1 Sound Card drill daily. The words with a schwa can be coded: **wăg ŏn**
                                                                                                                              c   c

Students may read a word with the expected short vowel sound rather than a schwa sound. For example, the word **seven** does have a schwa sound although the student might read the second **e** as short and decode the word without a problem. Do not consider this wrong! The goal of decoding has been achieved. *Do not mark the student wrong if he marks this word with a short vowel sound:* **sĕv ĕn** rather than **sĕv ĕn**
       c   c   c   c

PART 3

To practice the schwa sound, make schwa words on index cards and have students scoop the word into syllables. Pronounce the word and have the students repeat. Have them name the syllable with the schwa. They can cover the vowel with a little schwa card or write a schwa above the vowel.

PART 4   **PART 5**   **PART 6**

Follow the procedures for Parts 4, 5, and 6.

PART 7

After schwa is taught in Part 1, be sure to add that Sound Card when you spread them out for the student(s). Ask, "What says /ŭ/?" The response now will be "**u** and **ə** (schwa)." When the student points to the schwa card, ask, "What letters can make the schwa sound?" Response: "All the vowels" (**a**, **e**, **i**, **o** and **u**).

Schwa Spelling

Do not do this initially; wait several lessons. Teach to advanced and B level students only. Some A level students may be able to do this work, but dyslexic students should wait until further along in the program. Teachers can return to this when the students seem ready at a later point in the program.

Teach the student that the schwa vowel sound is hard to spell. Use Syllable Cards and the vowel Sound Cards, including the schwa card to practice these words. Place two blank Syllable Cards on the table or magnetic board. Spread out the vowel cards and the schwa card.

- Say the word as pronounced and have student repeat: /**wagən**/

- Have the student place the schwa card on the syllable that contains the schwa ⬚ə

- Then say the word the way that it is **spelled**, pronouncing the vowel sound: /**wăgŏn**/. Let the student repeat. Have the student replace the schwa card with the correct vowel card and spell the word by syllable. To reinforce the correct spelling, the student should use his index finger and middle finger to write the word on the tabletop, naming letters as he writes.

- This is also a nice time to introduce the student(s) to Dictionary/Spell Checker work. Dyslexic students benefit when initial dictionary work is introduced with a spell checker along with a dictionary. Some spell checkers come with a spell checker and a dictionary. The spell checker references the page number in the dictionary where the word can be found. This is ideal.

To use the spell checker and dictionary: Use Syllable Cards and the vowel Sound Cards, including the schwa card to practice these words. Place two Syllable Cards on the table or magnetic board. Spread out the vowel cards and the schwa card.

- Say the word as pronounced and have student repeat: /**wagǝn**/

- Have the student place the schwa card on the syllable that contains the schwa. Have the student spell the word by syllable, saying "schwa" where the schwa appears. In other words, the student says, "**wag**: **w** - **a** - **g**, **ǝn**: **ǝ** (schwa) - **n**." That spelling should then be entered into the spell checker, with the schwa represented with the letter **u**. The student can then be taught how to use the spell checker to find out which vowel is the correct one.

PART 8   PART 9   PART 10   Follow the procedures for Parts 8, 9, and 10.

3.2   What to Teach

- Decoding two closed syllables with more than three sounds in a syllable

- Syllable division principles

- Spelling multisyllabic words with more than three sounds in a syllable

Additional Materials Needed
- 3.2 Syllable Cards, 3.2 Word Cards

PART 1   Follow the procedure for Part 1

PART 2   Tell students that the words in 3.2 are similar to 3.1 words. Now, 3.2 words include blends, whereas 3.1 words did not have any blends. Show this on the table using the Sound Cards (**gumdrop**). Before you divide the word, ask the student whether or not it should be split. Review that it should be split if the vowels are separated. The peach vowel cards will help the student quickly and easily see that the vowels are separated. Model "scooping" the syllables with your finger as you read the word and let the students do the same. Have the student read each part and then read them together. Separate the cards into syllables: **gum drop**. The student should find the blend. Review the meaning of blend. Remind your students that a blend or digraph may be at the beginning or the end of any syllable. Demonstrate other words such as: **chil dren**, **pump kin** and **prob lem**. Divide the words into parts for the student and locate the blends.

This section adds the following syllable division rules:

1   If there are 3 consonants between vowels (without a digraph), the blend stays together.

2   If a blend can be made in both directions, almost always, the blend goes with the second syllable, (**hundred** - even though **nd** is a blend as well as **dr**, the blend stays together in the second syllable **hun dred**). Demonstrate this with Sound Cards on the table. Have students practice with other examples. A word is usually a compound word if the blend stays together in the first syllable (**sandlot**). Split between the two words.

3   When there are four consonants together, the blend will be split between them. Keep welded sounds, digraphs and blends together (**hand clasp**, **gang plank**).

Notebook Entry
(Syllable Section) Add 3.2 syllable division rules.

PART 3   Add new Word Cards. Continue to review a varied selection of words from other Substeps. Students should make additional Word Cards as needed. Make Word Cards with two syllables written in two different colors to aid students if needed.

A student needs to quickly divide words in his head in order to read fluently. Much practice is needed. Present the Word Cards from Substeps 3.1 and 3.2. Using both real and nonsense words, time the student as you present them as flashcards. Cover up the second syllable to assist as needed. Students may be timed in every lesson to increase speed. Tell them to read each part and not to look at the whole word and guess. Have the student scoop syllables with finger or pen point.

Follow the procedures for Parts 4, 5, and 6.

 Select words to use from the Dictation Book Substep (A or B vocabulary). Also, select words from the previous Substeps for review. When reviewing one-syllable words, students should make the words with Sound Cards or blank cards. Continue the multisyllabic spelling procedure using 3.2 Syllable Cards (see Part 7 in Substep 3.1 to review this process).

Continue to practice and reinforce the spelling of words that end with **ic**.

Most students have difficulty spelling words that begin with **ex**. They usually want to spell **extent** as **xstent**. First, use the Sound Cards to teach that the letter **e** is needed to say /**e**/ since the **x** just says /**ks**/. Then teach that the /**s**/ is "built in" to the sound of **x** (/**ks**/) so the letter **s** is not needed.

Be aware of another common difficulty: words that have a first syllable that sounds like a letter (such as **entrust**). Some of these words will be in this Substep. Others will not appear until later. A word such as **entrust** will be very difficult. Use the Sound Cards to explain the need for the first **e**. Practice these by dictating a nonsense syllable (**em**, **en**, **ex**).

   Follow the procedures for Parts 8, 9, and 10.

Include Review

Notes / FYI
Blends occur when two or more consonants are together within the same syllable, each making a sound. Thus, the **mp** in the word **pump kin** is a blend but the **mp** in the word **trum pet** is not a blend. The consonants must be in the same syllable to form a blend.

The schwa sound /ə/ can occur in any unaccented syllable. Only words with schwa in the second syllable are classified in the wordlists. A schwa in the first syllable is usually easy to decode, but can cause a problem for spelling. Examples include **complex**, **address** and **assist**. The schwa in the first syllable occurs in prefixes when combined with a root. The root is the stressed syllable. For now, students may be taught to spell some of these words with the same method used to teach schwa in Step 3.1. Words with double consonants (**assist**, **address**) occur when the last consonant in the prefix changes to match the first consonant in the Latin root (see Appendix). These words are decodable at this Substep; however, the spelling is enhanced by an understanding of morphological study of prefixes and roots. This advanced concept is presented in Step 12. Now, these words appear for reading, but not for spelling.

Helpful Hints / Activities
Make a match game with 3.2 words (see Helpful Hints / Activities 3.1)

3.3   What to Teach

- Reading and spelling words with the ct blend.

Additional Materials Needed

- 3.3 Word Cards, 3.3 Syllable Cards

PART 1   Follow the procedure for Part 1

PART 2   Tell the student that this Substep teaches **ct**, a difficult blend. Make the word subject with Sound Cards. Explain that the last syllable has a **ct** blend which requires practice. Be sure the student clearly says /**t**/; many leave off this sound. Explain that /**kt**/ is always spelled with **ct**. Words with **inct** are the most difficult and appear only in 3.3 B. Show students that these words have the **ink** + **t** sounds, using the green **ink** card. However, /**kt**/ uses a **c** rather than a **k** (**distinct**, **extinct**, **instinct**).

Syllable Division

Words with four consonants together can have a 3-letter blend. These stay together in the second syllable. Demonstrate with words such as **construct** and **obstruct**.

Notebook Entry

(Syllable Section) Add the 3.3 syllable division rule.

PART 3   **PART 4**   **PART 5**   **PART 6**   Follow the procedures for Part 3, 4, 5, and 6.

PART 7   For spelling, tell the student that whenever the word has /**kt**/ at the end, it is always spelled with **ct** - never **kt**. Be sure that the student listens carefully for the /**kt**/ sound and repeats the words accurately. The emphasis in this Substep is on the **ct** blend.

Notebook Entry

(Spelling Rules) Add the **ct** spelling to "Ways to spell /**k**/"

PART 8   **PART 9**   **PART 10**   Follow the procedures for Parts 8, 9, and 10.

Weave with Questions

Weave concepts, asking questions such as:

"What letters make the /**kt**/ blend?"

"Which words have a **ct** blend?"

"What is the blend in the last syllable?"

"How do you spell /**kt**/?"

"Where do you divide this word?"

3.4 What to Teach

- Three or four syllables can be put together to form multisyllabic words

- How to read and spell multisyllabic words with closed syllables

Additional Materials Needed
- 3.4 Word Cards, 3.4 Syllable Cards

PART 1

Follow the procedure for Part 1

PART 2

This Substep presents words with three or more closed syllables. Teach the student that words can contain three or more syllables combined. These longer words, when broken into parts, are quite easy for reading and spelling. Syllable division rules taught in Steps 3.1, 3.2 and 3.3 are applied in multisyllabic words. Use Sound Cards to demonstrate syllable division for selected words such as **snapdragon**, **fantastic**, and **athletic**. Use colored index cards (peach for vowels and white for consonants) for additional letters as needed. Then present the words with the Syllable Cards. Discuss syllable division. The student should read each syllable to form the longer words.

PART 3

If needed initially, make Word Cards with syllables divided. The student can do this as well for practice: | **fan tas tic** |

PART 4   **PART 5**   **PART 6**   **PART 7**

Follow the procedures for Part 4, 5, 6, and 7.

Remind students that multisyllabic words, ending in /ik/, are spelled **ic** (**fantastic**, **Atlantic**). Use 3.4 Syllable Cards to practice words for spelling. Be sure students spell one syllable at a time.

PART 8   **PART 9**   **PART 10**

Follow the procedures for Parts 8, 9, and 10.

Helpful Hints / Activities

The students can use sentence pages in the reader to find and underline the syllables in multisyllabic words. For example:

Mr. Smith is the **con** **gress** **man** for this **dis** **trict**.

Weave with Questions

"Where do you divide this word?"

3.5   What to Teach

- Two new suffix endings: -**ing** and -**ed** (/ĕd/ sound only)
- The suffixes are added to **unchanging** basewords from Steps 1, 2 and 3.

Additional Materials Needed

- Suffix Cards -**ing** and -**ed**, yellow Syllable Cards and 3.5 Word Cards

PART 1   Follow the procedure for Part 1.

PART 2   The student will learn about suffixes. Tell the student that endings can be added to a baseword to make longer words. Demonstrate with the word **bug** on the table. Add **s** to form **bugs**. **Bug** is the baseword and **s** is added to it; **s** is a suffix. A **suffix** is an ending that can be added to a baseword. There are two kinds, **vowel** suffixes begin with vowels and **consonant** suffixes begin with consonants.

Explain that the suffixes -**ed** and -**ing** are both vowel suffixes (they begin with a vowel) as you display them on Suffix Cards. Make large index cards with basewords such as **rent** and **inspect** or use appropriate Word Cards from previous steps. Add the suffix -**ing** (**rent** + **ing**). Have the student read the baseword, then the entire word with baseword and suffix together: **rent** - **renting**. Ask, "What is the baseword? What is the suffix?" Do the same with -**ed**. Instruct the student to read these words naming just the baseword first, then the baseword + suffix. This helps them solidify the concept and also prepares them for spelling.

PART 3   Add new Word Cards. Continue to review a varied selection of words from other Substeps. Students should make additional Word Cards as needed. The student should make a personal set of 3.5 words to mark-up. Teach them to underline or scoop the baseword and circle the suffix:

PART 4   **PART 5**   **PART 6**      **PART 7**   Follow the procedures for Part 4, 5, 6 and 7. The student must spell the baseword first. When **publishing** is dictated, the student must first repeat the word (**publishing**), name the baseword (**publish**), spell this by syllables, (**pub lish**), and then add the suffix, (-**ing**). Use blank index cards to represent syllables in the baseword and the -**ed** and -**ing** Suffix Cards for the student to pull down and then spell the word. It is vital that you establish the habit of naming and spelling the baseword before adding the suffix. **Notebook Entry** (Spelling Section) Add the -**ed** and -**ing** suffix to the Suffix Ending page.

PART 8   **PART 9**   **PART 10**   Follow the procedures for Parts 8, 9, and 10.

Notes / FYI

The -**ed** suffix is taught further in Step 6. Currently, -**ed** says /ĕd/; later students learn that -**ed** says /**d**/ as in **spilled** and /**t**/ as in **swished**. Avoid these words now; only use /ĕd/ sound.

Weave with Questions

"What is the baseword?" and "What is the suffix?" Teach students to underline the basewords and circle the suffix: **rent** (ed)   **fin ish** (ing)

Step 4

At the end of this step, students should know:

- The description of a vowel-consonant-e syllable and how to mark these syllables
- The difference between a closed and a vowel-consonant-e syllable
- Long vowel sounds, including the two long sounds for **u**
- **s** between two vowels may say **/z/**
- How to read and spell a vowel-consonant-e syllable, alone or combined with closed syllables
- Words do not end in **v**; an **e** will always follow

Students have mastered closed syllables in three steps. In addition to mastering closed syllables with short vowels, the goals of Steps 1-3 include the thorough understanding and application of sound segmentation and syllable segmentation. This is more manageable for students when applying these essential skills to only one syllable type. Now that sound and syllable segmentation are firm, the student is ready to add another syllable type. The next one to be added is a pattern often familiar to many students, the vowel-consonant-e (v-e) syllable.

Initially, the new syllable type is presented in isolation. Then, the v-e syllable is combined with closed syllables to form multisyllabic words. Lastly, a vowel-consonant-e exception is taught.

4.1 What to Teach

- Vowel-consonant-e syllable

- Long vowel sounds and new keywords

- Two sounds for the vowel **u**

- /**z**/ sound of **s** between two vowels

Additional Materials Needed

- 4.1 Word Cards

- Step 4 Student Reader and Student Rules Notebook

- Student Workbook 4A (optional)

PART 1

a

For the first lesson in Step 4, skip to Part 2 and return here after you teach about vowel-consonant-e syllables.

Hold up the vowel cards in order. Tell the student that **a** says /ā/ as in **safe**. Have student repeat letter, keyword, and sound: **a - safe** - /ā/. Point out that this long sound is simply the name of the letter. Repeat for every vowel and when you get to **u**, explain that **u** is the only vowel that has two long sounds: /ū/ as in mule and /ü/ as in **rule**. Explain that sometimes it is difficult to get the whole **u** to come out smoothly so part of the sound /ū/ is "chopped off" and it sounds like /ü/. Have the student listen to hear the difference. Tap out **rule** and **mule**, stopping at the sound of **u**. Go through the vowel cards again.

Students must now say the following for vowels: "**a - apple** - /ă/, **a - safe** - /ā/." Teachers should model this until students can do it independently. When students learn about **s** between vowels, they should say "**s - snake** - /s/, **s - wise** -/z/" or "**s** /s/, /z/" during the drill.

Notebook Entry

(Sound Section) Add vowel-consonant-e page with keywords. Add the *Jobs of Silent* **e** on the same page. Add the keyword **wise** to the sound of **s** to represent the /**z**/ sound when **s** is between two vowels. This belongs on the consonant page.

PART 2

In this Substep, a new syllable type is taught: vowel-consonant-e. Review closed syllable with student using Sound Cards on the table. Now use Sound Cards to make the word **hop**. Let the student tap out the sounds and tell how many sounds are in the word (three). Next, have the students listen to you tap the word **hope**. Explain that the word **hope** also has three sounds, but the **o** says its name instead of /ŏ/ as in **octopus**. The way to make it do that is to add an **e**. Add **e** to make the word **hope**. Tap it out again. Tell the student that **e** is "the busiest letter in the alphabet." It constantly volunteers to help out and often "keeps its mouth closed" while it works. **E** is overworked and underpaid, but it doesn't seem to mind. The **e** in hope is silent. It jumps over the **p** to give **o** the long sound. **O** says /ō/ when it is long. Put **cap** out. Ask the student to tap sounds and name the word. Ask him to make it into the word **cape** (add **e**). Tap out **cape**: /k/ /ā/ /p/. It has only three sounds and the **a** is long. Point out the **a**-consonant-e. Tell students that whenever there is a vowel, then a consonant, then an **e** at the end of the syllable, the **e** is silent and the vowel says its name (the long sound). The **e** can jump over one sound to change the vowel from a short sound to a long sound. Tell students that whenever a vowel-consonant-e situation appears in a syllable, it is not a closed syllable. This is the second kind of syllable; the vowel-consonant-e syllable. Show students how to mark this syllable: **m ā k e̸**
v-e

Use the Sound Cards to practice reading one-syllable closed versus v-e words. Students should practice with both real and nonsense pairs (**cap** - **cape**, **fat** - **fate**, **tape** - **tap**, **lat** - **late**, **gobe** - **gob**, etc.). Sufficient practice with the Sound Cards is important in every lesson. It is often helpful to let the student tap again in order to master the new syllable type.

Show students the word **rise** and **wise**. Teach that **s** might say /**z**/ between two vowels. Students should be asked, "When can **s** say /**z**/?" and the response should be, "As a suffix or when between two vowels."

Even though this is called vowel-consonant-e, the **e** can actually "jump over" a digraph as well. Examples are **bathe** and **clothe**. Demonstrate using Sound Cards.

In subsequent lessons, after the student has mastered the v-e pattern, use the Sound Cards to demonstrate words with the suffix -**s** added (**cakes**, **hopes**, etc.) These should be read: **cake** - **cakes**. The suffix -**s** is circled.

Notebook Entry
(Syllable Section) Add the definition of a vowel-consonant-e syllable.

PART 3 Add 4.1 Word Cards and try these activities:

- Have students read cards in the following manner: cover up **e**, read the word (**lim**), uncover **e** and read the word (**lime**).

- Students can categorize closed and v-e syllables into two groups.

- Students can make more 4.1 Word Cards and mark them appropriately.

- Students can make Word Cards with the vowels written in peach and the consonants written in black. This helps to emphasize the v-e pattern.

PART 4 Substep 4.1 offers varied wordlists in the Student Readers. Review them before using with students, particularly the adding of suffix -**s**. These more challenging wordlists should be read before the student moves on to 4.2.

PART 5 Follow the procedures for Part 5.

PART 6 Teach the response to "What says /**ā**/?" (a-consonant-e). Review with Sound Cards how **e** helps to change a vowel from a short sound in **hop** to a long sound in **hope**. Tap it out. The **e** is not heard, but it has to be there to make the **o** say its name.

Spread out the vowel cards and a blank ivory card. Make an additional **e** card with a peach index card or construction paper. Ask, "What says /**ō**/?" Demonstrate that **o** says /**ō**/ when it is followed by a consonant (use blank card) and an **e**.

Explain that the blank card represents a consonant. Cover the blank card with various consonants such as **t**, **m**, **p** or **f** and have the students read: **ote**, **ome**, **ope**, **ofe**. Return to the blank card and repeat that the blank card stands for a consonant. Ask, "What says /ī/?" Have students place the cards:

The oral answer should also be given as the student points to the cards, "**i** - consonant - **e**." Demonstrate how to write this: **i** - **e**, etc. The dash stands in the place of the blank card and represents a consonant. An oral answer should also be given when a student writes: "**i** - consonant - **e**." Be sure to ask "What says /ū/?" and "What says /ü/?"

PART 7   Use Sound Cards for students to spell 4.1 words. Dictate the word, have the student repeat and then find the Sound Cards to spell the word. Blank cards may be used for consonants. Be sure to dictate closed syllables as well, so that you can teach the student to listen for the long or short sound.

Be sure v-e words with the suffix -**s** are dictated for spelling prior to moving on to 4.2.

PART 8   **PART 9**   **PART 10**   Follow the procedures for Parts 8, 9, and 10.

Helpful Hints / Activities

Use index cards to make the following Word Cards: **cop**, **cap**, **hop**, **pal**, **cod**, **hat**, **mat**, **tap**, **dud**, **cut**, **slid**, **sham**, **fin**, **dim**, **spit**, **slop**, **rob**, **not**, **cub**, **tot**. Present one at a time. Read **cap**; then add **e** and read **cape**.

Weave with Questions

"Is this word a closed or vowel-consonant-e syllable?"

"What does the vowel say in this word?"

"What does the **e** say?"

Find any vowel-consonant-e words

Students mark these syllables: **h ō p e**
                               v-e

Explain that the **v** stands for vowel, and the **-** stands for consonant (vowel-consonant-e)

4.2   What to Teach

- Combining closed syllables with vowel-consonant-e syllables to form words with two syllables

- Compound words with vowel-consonant-e syllable in the first syllable

Additional Materials Needed

- 4.2 Word Cards, 4.2 Syllable Cards

PART 1   Follow the procedure for Part 1.

PART 2   Teach how to combine closed and v-e syllables. Explain to the student that closed syllables and vowel-consonant-e syllables can be combined together to form longer words. Use the Step 4.2 Syllable Cards to demonstrate. For example, make the word | **ath** | **lete** |. Discuss each syllable, including the vowel sound. Explain that this Substep presents words with closed and v-e syllables. Now use the Sound Cards to make the word | a | d | m | i | r | e |. Have the student separate it into two syllables and then read it. Explain that the previous syllable division rules apply. Make the word | f | i | r | e | m | an | and divide it into syllables. Let the student read it. Explain that compound words can begin with a v-e syllable. Use Syllable Cards to practice other 4.2 words. Students must learn to divide words and then read them.

PART 3   Add 4.2 Word Cards. Teach students to mark syllables:

c = closed (˘) breve   **v-e** = vowel-consonant-e (¯) macron

After they've underlined or scooped syllables in a word, they mark the syllables:

rĕp tīle
 c   v-e

PART 4   **PART 5**   **PART 6**   Follow the procedures for Parts 4, 5, and 6.

Note for Part 4: Compound words are listed first. Be sure to also use the other lists.

PART 7   Be sure to use Syllable Cards. Have student name and spell one syllable at a time.

PART 8   **PART 9**   **PART 10**   Follow the procedures for Parts 8, 9, and 10.

Helpful Hints / Activities

Mark multisyllabic words in sentences. For example:

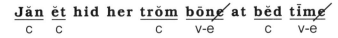

Jăn ĕt hid her trŏm bōne at bĕd tīme
 c   c   c   v-e   c   v-e

Use Syllable Cards to make a match game (see Helpful Hints / Activities, Step 3.1)

4.3　What to Teach

- Combining closed syllables with vowel-consonant-e syllables to form multisyllabic words

Additional Materials Needed

- 4.3 Word Cards, 4.3 Syllable Cards

 PART 1　Follow the procedure for Part 1.

 PART 2　Tell students that three and four syllables can be combined to form longer words. Use the Syllable Cards to make the word: | **val** | **en** | **tine** |

Have the student read each syllable and then combine them to pronounce the word. It is helpful to "scoop" the syllables with the index finger as the word is read. Present additional words using Syllable Cards. Discuss syllables and vowel sounds.

 PART 3　Add 4.3 Word Cards. Make more Word Cards with syllables in two different colors to aid students, if needed.

Combine Step 4.3 Word Cards with those of previous steps. Time students as words are read, increasing speed in subsequent lessons.

 PART 4　Students can mark the syllables on a personal set of Word Cards. Students may try to divide and read words on their own. If they have difficulty, work it out with them.

 PART 5　 **PART 6**　**PART 7**　Follow the procedures for Parts 5, 6, and 7.

 PART 8　 **PART 9**　 **PART 10**　Follow the procedures for Parts 8, 9, and 10.

 Weave with Questions

Continue with, "Find the v-e syllables"

Ask, "How many syllables in this word?"

4.4   What to Teach

- Words do not end in **v**; silent **e** always ends words for **v**.

Additional Materials Needed
- Green **ive** Sound Card
- 4.4 Word Cards, 4.4 Syllable Cards

PART 1

Students learn the exception to the vowel-consonant-e rule involving the letter **v**: No word ends in **v**.

Review closed syllable with Sound Cards on the table. Ask the student to name exceptions to this rule (this should be no problem if it has been reviewed often). Display the green **ild**, **ind**, **old**, **ost**, **olt** cards.

Skip to Part 2. In subsequent lessons, students should say, "**ive** - **give** - /ĭv/" for the Sound Card drill.

PART 2

Use Sound Cards to review the v-e syllable. Tell the student that this syllable also has an exception. Teach that there are some letters in the alphabet that refuse to be at the end of a word (*even letters hate being at the end of the line!*). One of these is the letter **v**. Put the following Sound Cards on the table: g i v . Have the student tap this out and name the word (**give**). Explain that it says /gĭv/, but that v refuses to be at the end. Ask the student to guess which letter volunteers to help out (**e**). Good ol' **e** again! In this case, the **e** is there for the **v**. It does not make the **i** long. Replace the individual cards with the green **ive** card. Teach the keyword. Sometimes, the letter **e** does two jobs, as in the word **five**. The words **live** and **live** are spelled the same way: in one word, the **e** has two jobs; in the other the **e** is just there for the **v**. Tell students that the words in Step 4.4 have a vowel-consonant-e, but that the **e** is at the end for the letter **v**. Use Syllable Cards to practice additional words such as ol ive .

PART 3

Add 4.4 Word Cards and teach students how to mark the v-e exception:

Notebook Entry
(Syllable Section) Add the vowel-consonant-e exception. Add the second **job of silent e** to the Sound Section.

PART 4   **PART 5**

Follow the procedures for Parts 4 and 5.

PART 6

Be sure to now ask "What Says /ĭv/?" (**ive**).

PART 7

Use the green Sound Card and a blank consonant card to dictate the words **give**, **have**, and **lĭve**. Have the students repeat the word, find cards, and then spell orally. Use Syllable Cards to spell multisyllabic words.

PART 8   **PART 9**   **PART 10**   Follow the procedures for Parts 8, 9, and 10.

Notes / FYI

Some closed syllables also end with the /**v**/ sound; the **v** is followed by a silent **e** in these words too. Some examples are: **twelve**, **solve**, **delve**, **shelve**, **valve**, **dissolve**, **involve**, **absolve**, etc. This can be taught to **advanced** students. Use Sound Cards to demonstrate.

These words are marked as closed syllables. They are *not* closed syllable exceptions since the vowel has the expected short sound. The silent **e**, however should be crossed out: **twĕlve**
c

At this point in the program, let the student read and spell words by dividing them into syllables. Later, they will learn that **ive** is often a suffix added to a baseword.

Weave with Questions

"What letter never ends a word?"
"Why is the **e** at the end of a word?"

Step 5

At the end of this step, students should know:

- The description of an open syllable and how to mark these syllables

- The difference between open, closed and vowel-consonant-e syllables

- **y** as a vowel in an open syllable has two sounds: /ī/ and /ē/

- How to read and spell an open syllable, alone or combined with closed and/or vowel-consonant-e syllables

- Syllable division principles with open syllables

- Schwa vowel sound in unstressed, open syllables

Students will learn the third type of syllable common in English words: the Open Syllable. Initially, the new syllable type is presented in isolation. Then it is combined with the two other known types of syllables (closed and v-e). One of the most important concepts taught in Step 5 is flexibility with syllable division. This must be practiced with Sound Cards in Step 5.2. The letter **y** is taught as a vowel in open syllables with the sounds /ī/ and /ē/. Lastly, students learn exceptions to the open syllable with the schwa sound found in unaccented syllables.

5.1 What to Teach

- Reading and spelling of open syllables and how to mark them

- **y** as a vowel in an open syllable has two sounds: /ī/ and /ē/

Additional Materials Needed

- **y** vowel (peach) Sound Card

- 5.1 Word Cards

- Step 5 Student Reader and Student Rules Notebook

- Student Workbook 5A (optional)

PART 1

Omit this part of the lesson until after you teach about open syllables in Part 2.

Teach the keywords for the open syllable vowel sounds:

a - **acorn** - /ā/, **e** - **me** - /ē/, **i** - **hi** - /ī/, **o** - **no** - /ō/, **u** - **pupil** - /ū/, **u** - **flu** - /ü/

New vowel sound: **y** - **cry** - /ī/

Now students should add the open syllable response to the vowel card drill. Model each vowel and have the student repeat: **a** - **apple** - /ă/, **a** - **safe** - /ā/, **a** - **acorn** - /ā/

This stands for "**a** says /ă/ as in **apple**, **a** says /ā/ as in **safe**, and **a** says /ā/ as in **acorn**."

Notebook Entry

(Sound Section) Add the long vowel sounds in open syllables for Step 5.1 only.

PART 2

The students will learn the open syllable concept and **y** as a vowel. Put Sound Cards on the table to form the word **hit**. Ask students, "What kind of syllable is that?" (closed). Ask, "Why is it closed?" (one vowel closed in by a consonant). Now ask, "What sound does the vowel make?" (short). Ask the students if they know how to make the syllable open, rather than closed (remove **t**). "If closed makes the vowel short," you ask, "what sound will an open syllable have?" (long). Read the word **hi**. Explain that open syllables have only one vowel - and that vowel is left open. It must be the last letter in the syllable. Use Sound Cards on the table to read several real and nonsense words with **a**, **e**, **i**, **o**, **u** in open syllables (one syllable only). Have students name the two long sounds of **u** (/ū/, /ü/). Explain that, as in v-e syllables, **u** might have either sound in an open syllable.

Put the word **my** on the table. Be sure to use the vowel (peach) Sound Card for **y** and not the ivory colored consonant card. Most students will read this word correctly. Tell them that **y** is sometimes a vowel in an open syllable. When it is in a one-syllable word, **y** says /ī/ in an open syllable.

Tell the students that the vowel might be the only letter in the syllable. It is then a single vowel (not closed in), so it is long (ex. **I**).

Notebook Entry

(Syllable Section) Copy the definition and examples of open syllable.

PART 3

Teach students how to mark open syllables:

prō

o

Follow the procedures for Parts 4 and 5.

 Spread out the vowel cards, including the **y** vowel card and a blank consonant card. Ask, "What says /ō/?"

The student should pull down $\boxed{o}$ and answer, "**o** in an open syllable" and then also put together $\boxed{o}$ $\boxed{}$ $\boxed{e}$ and say, "**o**-consonant-**e**." The response for "What says /ī/?" should now include the **y** vowel card (**i**, **i** - **e**, **y**).

 For Spelling, tell the student that one-syllable words ending in the sound /ī/, are spelled with **y**, rather than **i** (except **pi** and **hi**). Dictate words and nonsense syllables. Students should use Sound Cards to spell these words (blank cards may be used for consonants). Be sure to dictate review words as well as open syllables.

   Follow the procedures for Parts 8, 9, and 10.

 Helpful Hints / Activities
Put Sound Cards on the table to form nonsense syllables, changing from open to closed to v-e, and vice versa. For example, start with **sti**, change to **stib**, add **e** for **stibe**. Then change **b** to **m** for **stime**, remove **e** to make **stim**, and remove **m** to return to **sti**. Repeat with a new syllable base, such as **flo**. Let student read each as quickly as possible and discuss differences between syllables.

Dictate Step 5.1 real and nonsense syllables combined with some from Step 2 and Step 4.1. Have students spell the words, listing them in the appropriate column, then mark syllable type and vowel sound. For example:

Closed	Vowel-Consonant-e	Open
belt (Step 2.2)	**slīde** (Step 4.1)	**mē** (Step 5.1)
c	v-e	o

 Weave with Questions
"What kind of syllable is this?"
"What does that tell you about the vowel?"
Find any open syllables. Mark open syllables.

5.2   What to Teach

- Combining open syllables with closed and v-e syllables to form two-syllable words

- Syllable division principles with open syllables

- Flexibility with syllable division

Additional Materials Needed
- 5.2 Syllable Cards, 5.2 Word Cards

PART 1

This stands for "**a** says /ă/ as in **apple**, **a** says /ā/ as in **safe**, and **a** says /ā/ as in **acorn**."

PART 2

Tell the student that many, many words are made with open syllables. Use Syllable Cards to demonstrate. Sometimes an open syllable is combined with a closed syllable, as in **si lent**. It is also combined with vowel-consonant-e syllables, such as **lo cate**.

There are new syllable division rules to be taught. Explain that when one consonant is between two vowels, the consonant might close in the first syllable or it might go with the second syllable, leaving the first one open. Use Sound Cards to compare two words such as **relish** and **protect**. Make the word **relish** with the Sound Cards. Ask students to divide the word. Discuss the syllable division rule that puts the **l** with the first syllable to close it in. Explain that with the open syllable, the consonant may go with the second syllable instead, leaving the first syllable open. Demonstrate with the word **protect**.

Students must learn to be flexible and thus if one-syllable division does not seem to make a word, the other must be tried. Students must learn to try both ways that a word might be read. The consonant more often goes with the second syllable so that division should be attempted first. Students will only recognize the correct division if the word is familiar. Only after students are familiar with the word will they know which is the correct pronunciation. The students need to master the flexibility of trying both sounds. This should be continually practiced with the Sound Cards.

When students have worked sufficiently with one consonant syllable division, the next principle can be explained. Use the Syllable Cards to display the word **pro gram** and let students read it. Next, make the same word with the Sound Cards. Split the word into syllables for the students. Point out (by moving the **g** card) that the **gr** blend stays together in the second syllable rather than splitting between the two consonants. Now that the open syllable is known, explain that sometimes a blend stays together in the second syllable, leaving the first syllable open. This usually occurs when the first syllable is a prefix such as **re-**, **pro-**, **pre-**, etc.

Tell students that open syllables can also be the last syllable in a word, as in **limbo** and **bingo**. Lastly, if **y** ends the first syllable in a word, it says /ī/, as in **sky line**.

Notebook Entry
(Syllable Section) Add that "these syllables can be combined with others to form longer words" to the open syllable page. Add the Rules for Syllable Division for Step 5.2.

PART 3

Make words with syllables in two colors, if necessary. Students should make a personal set of 5.2 Word Cards to scoop syllables and mark. Students may also use their own Word Cards to make Syllable Cards. Let students say where they are going to divide and then literally cut them into two syllables.

PART 4 If a student is charting in Part 4 of the lesson and reads a word incorrectly (**mŏm ent**) then it is not counted as an error if the student gets the word when the teacher says, "How else could you divide and read that word?"

PART 5 **PART 6** Follow the procedures for Parts 5 and 6.

PART 7 Be sure the student spells one syllable at a time. Some open syllables within words are real words that use a vowel digraph. For example: **fre quent**; the student may know how to spell the word **free**. If he spells the first syllable **free**, say, "That is the word **free**; how do you spell the open syllable /**fre**/?"

PART 8 **PART 9** **PART 10** Follow the procedures for Parts 8, 9, and 10.

Helpful Hints / Activities

Find words from Step 3.1 and 3.2 that have one consonant closing in the first vowel. Make a list and mix them with Step 5.2 words that have one consonant in the middle of the word going with the second syllable. Tell the student to underline the syllables, deciding whether the first syllable is closed or open.

ro dent	mi nus	sev enth	be gin
O C	O C	C C	O C
tu lip	cab in	tal ent	re mote
O C	C C	C C	O C

Use two different colored, transparent plastic rectangles, taped together. Place over words on the wordlist to help determine syllable division. Make nonsense words with Sound Cards, such as **robelt**. Let the student divide and read the nonsense word in two different ways to practice flexibility.

An electronic spell checker and/or dictionary is useful with this step. Students can check syllable division for unknown words and then pronounce the word when the vowel sound has been determined.

As in Step 3, advanced students may benefit from further morphological study. This is helpful for two reasons: vocabulary development and syllable division. See the Appendix of this manual for resource suggestions.

Weave with Questions

"Where will you divide this word?"

If presenting nonsense words, ask, "How else can you divide it?"

If working with real words and student divides incorrectly, ask, "How else can you divide it?" and "How is it pronounced now?"

Help the student determine the correct answer.

5.3   What to Teach

- **y** - **y** says /ē/ - as a vowel at the end of multisyllabic words

- How to read and spell words ending with the vowel **y**

Additional Materials Needed
- 5.3 Syllable Cards, 5.3 Word Cards

- White index cards

PART 1

Skip Part 1 of the lesson until after you teach y as a vowel at the end of multisyllabic words in Part 2.

Teach the new keyword **baby** for the /ē/ sound of **y**. Student response to the **y** vowel during the quick drill should now be "**y** - **cry** - /ī/ and **y** - **baby** - /ē/."

Notebook Entry
(Sound Section) Add the keyword **baby** to the open syllable vowel page.

PART 2

Remind the student that **y** can sometimes be a vowel. Demonstrate with the word **try**. It is open, so it is long. Review that **y** in an open syllable in a one-syllable word has the long sound /ī/. Now add **pan** to form the word **pantry**. Tell the student that **y** in an open syllable at the end of a multisyllabic word usually says /ē/.

It is still open and has a long sound, but most often, it is not long /ī/, it is long /ē/. Use Step 5.3 Syllable Cards to demonstrate this concept further.

PART 3

Teach how to mark the open syllable ending with a **y**: **pĕn nȳ**

                                  c   o

The student may also put an /ē/ above the **y** to indicate its sound.

PART 4   **PART 5**

Follow the procedures for Parts 4 and 5.

PART 6

Spread out vowel cards and a blank consonant card. Make an additional **e** vowel card from a peach index card or construction paper. Ask, "What says /ē/?"

The student should pull down **e** and say "**e** in an open syllable," **e** - blank - **e** and say "**e** - consonant - **e**," and **y** and say "**y** at the end of a multisyllabic word."

PART 7 For Spelling, tell the student that at the end of a multisyllabic word, /ē/ is spelled with **y**. (Later in the program, he will learn other spellings). If a student spells a word with **ey** at the end, tell him that **ey** says /ē/ as well, but it is less common than **y** and it will be taught later.

Many multisyllabic words ending in **y** have two consonants. Put out the Sound Cards: **buny**. Review that the consonant **n** might go with the first syllable: <u>**bun**</u> y or with the second syllable: **bu** <u>**ny**</u>. Tell the student that the words with a short vowel get an extra consonant: **bun ny** (make another **n** on a white index card). This helps close in the first vowel to make it short. Have a stack of blank white index cards. Dictate words with short and long sounds (short: **penny** vs. long: **tiny**, **baby**). Have the student make the extra consonant card for words with short vowels.

(Note: Two words with short vowels that do not have double consonants are **study** and **copy**. Tell students "You should *study*, not *copy*.")

PART 8 **PART 9** **PART 10** Follow the procedures for Parts 8, 9, and 10.

Notes / FYI

Many words in 3.1 have double consonants such as **tennis** and **rabbit**. The extra consonant helps close in the first vowel. This can be explained now that the student has learned open (**tennis** vs. **tenis** and **rabbit** vs. **rabit**). The words with this extra consonant are similar to the 5.3 words that end in **y** (such as **bunny**). These words can be thought of as "bunny rabbit" words.

Notebook Entry

(Spelling Section) Add reasons to double consonants.

Y can say /ī/ at the end of a multisyllabic word, but most often it says /ē/. This will be taught in a later step since it is less common. Some examples: **rely**, **deny**, **July**.

Weave with Questions

"What does the **y** say?"

"Why are there two consonants in this word?"

5.4 What to Teach

- Reading and spelling open syllables combined with v-e and closed syllables in multisyllabic words.

Additional Materials Needed

- 5.4 Syllable Cards, 5.4 Word Cards

 PART 1 Follow the procedure for Part 1.

 PART 2 Tell students that open, closed, and vowel-consonant-e syllables can be combined to form multisyllabic words. The best way to demonstrate this is to use the three Syllable Cards:

gal	ax	y
im	po	lite
com	pre	hend

Have the student read the syllables separately, then combine them to form the real word. Then show **syllable division**, using the Sound Cards, applying principles and using flexibility as needed. The words in 5.4 are very difficult. You can initially divide these for the students in all parts of the lesson.

A student does not need to memorize syllable division rules. By doing it with Sound Cards, the student practices the principles. Remind them of the various "hints" as needed.

 PART 3 It is very helpful to make Word Cards with the word written on one side and then again on the reverse side, but with space between each syllable. The student initially reads the easier side (the divided side) and then flips it over to see the whole word. Eventually he does the harder side (undivided) first and if he's unable to get it, he can flip it over to see the word divided.

 PART 4 It is very helpful to have students underline syllables in a wordlist before reading. You might need to do this initially. A copy of one page in the Student Reader may be made for this purpose. It's good practice to mark some of the syllable types and vowels, but it's not necessary to do them all.

 PART 5 **PART 6** Follow the procedures for Parts 5 and 6.

 PART 7 The student must spell one syllable at a time! He should name each syllable. For example, if he spells **reg u**, then asks you for the last syllable - do not say "**late**". Rather, dictate the entire word, **regulate**, and ask *him* to name the syllable. Use Syllable Cards to practice spelling the words.

 PART 8 **PART 9** **PART 10** Follow the procedures for Parts 8, 9, and 10.

5.5   What to Teach

- The schwa (/ə/) sound for **a** in unstressed, open syllables

- The schwa (/ə/) sound for **i** in unstressed, open syllables

Additional Materials Needed

- Schwa vowel card

- 5.5 Syllable Cards, 5.5 Word Cards

PART 1

Skip Part 1 of the lesson until after you teach about the open syllable exceptions in Part 2. Teach the new, additional keywords for **a** and **i**:

a - Alaska - /ə/ say:"a - Alaska - a /ŭ/"   **i - compliment** - /ə/ say:"i - compliment - /ŭ/ or /ĭ/"

Notebook Entry

(Sound Section) Add these new keywords to the open syllable vowel page. Also, the sound options should be added to the sound option page.

PART 2

Remind the student that each syllable type has exceptions! Review **ild**, **old**, **ind**, **ost** and **olt** for closed syllables and words ending in **v** for vowel-consonant-e syllables, **ive**. Tell the student that open syllables have long vowels. The exception concerns two vowels: **a** and **i**. Use the Sound Cards to form the word: ⌐e⌐ ⌐x⌐ ⌐t⌐ ⌐r⌐ ⌐a⌐

Read it to the student. Ask what sound the **a** *should* make in an open syllable (/ā/).

Explain that in **extra**, **a** says /ŭ/ - it sounds like a short **u**. Cover the **a** with the schwa card. Tell the student that schwa says /ŭ/. We use the schwa card to show when a vowel makes an unexpected sound. We expect a to say /ā/ but it says /ŭ/. This happens whenever a ends a word in an open syllable. It also happens when a begins a word in an open syllable. The letter **a** in an unstressed, open syllable says /ŭ/. This usually occurs in the first or the last syllable in a word (**a lone**, **a maze**, **ex tra**). Use Sound Cards to practice. Cover the **a** with the schwa card and read the word. In subsequent lessons, after students have mastered words with the **a** exception, teach about the **i** exception.

Teach that when **i** is in an unstressed, open syllable, it does not make a long sound, as expected. Instead, it says /ŭ/ or /ĭ/. **This usually happens in the middle of a word**.

Use the Syllable Cards for ⌐com⌐ ⌐pli⌐ ⌐ment⌐. Cover the **i** with the schwa vowel card.

Since most students have trouble with accent, stress the **position** of the **a** and **i** rather than the syllable stress. However, the explanation should be given to the student that the schwa happens in the unstressed open syllable.

Notebook Entry

(Syllable Section) Add the Open Syllable Exception.

PART 3

Teach students how to mark this syllable exception:

WRS INSTRUCTOR MANUAL   **87**

PART 4   **PART 5** Follow the procedures for Parts 4 and 5.

 PART 6 Ask "What says /ŭ/?" (**u**, **ə**). Have them get the **u** and **ə** cards: Ask, "What letters say /ə/ in an open syllable?" (**a**, **i**). The sound /ŭ/ at the end of a syllable is always spelled with **a**.

PART 7 Use the Syllable Cards. Dictate a word, with the Syllable Cards turned over so that the blank side faces up: ☐ ☐ = | **ex** | **tra** |

Have the student place the ə on the syllable that has the schwa: | ☐ | ə |

The student must then name and spell one syllable at a time and then turn over the card to determine whether or not he spelled the word correctly.

| ☐ | ☐ | ☐ | for **compliment**: | ☐ | ə | ☐ |

 PART 8 **PART 9** **PART 10** Follow the procedures for Parts 8, 9, and 10.

 Helpful Hints / Activities
On the wordlists, students can put a **ə** above the unstressed **a** or the unstressed **i**. Review that it sounds like short **u**.

   ə   ə
A las ka　　　　**in di cate**
　　　　　　　　　　　ə

Notes / FYI
Schwa occurs in unaccented or unstressed syllables. Although schwa is not exactly the same sound as short **u** - /ŭ/ teaching this is the most effective way to succeed with students. Schwa is technically not a sound but a phonetic variant (when schwa occurs, the vowel is reduced to a less distinct form).

It is **not essential** that a student hear the unstressed syllable. Many people have difficulty hearing the difference between stressed and unstressed syllables. Therefore, it is important to teach the student the **position** where the unstressed open syllable occurs in a word.

It is **not necessary** to teach that the other vowels, **e**, **o**, **u**, often have a "half-long" sound in unstressed, open syllables. These words are easily decodable for reading and encodable for spelling.

Step 6

At the end of this step, students should know:

- Several suffixes beginning with a vowel and several beginning with a consonant
- How to read and spell words containing known syllables and suffixes when the baseword remains intact
- Three sounds of the -**ed** suffix
- The description of a consonant-le syllable
- The differences between closed, vowel-consonant-e, open and consonant-le syllables
- How to divide, read and spell words with a consonant-le syllable
- How to read and spell the exception to the consonant-le syllable, **stle**

Suffix work ranges from very simple to very complex, demanding a thorough understanding and application of language structure. The following words provide examples with progressively more difficult concepts.

- **hat** + **s** = **hats**, **bug** + **s** = **bugs**
- **hope** + **ful** = **hopeful**, **ship** + **ment** = **shipment**
- **hope** + **ing** = **hoping**, **top** + **ing** = **topping**
- **maniac** + **al** = **maniacal** (difficult for reading as well as spelling - baseword changes when suffix is added.

In the Wilson Reading System, work begins with the easy application of suffixes. This work began in Step 1 with the suffix -**s**. The -**ed** and -**ing** suffixes were added in Step 3. In Step 6, more suffixes are added to unchanging basewords. Be careful not to present words that require any changes to the basewords (**hope** + **ing** or **top** + **ing**). These are taught in a later step.

In Substep 6.4, a new syllable type is taught (consonant-le syllable). The four syllables learned in Steps 1-6 (closed, vowel-consonant-e, open and consonant-le) combine to form thousands of words. Students completing Steps 1-6 know how to segment and blend up to six sounds in a syllable. They know the principles of syllable division and the common suffixes.

6.1   What to Teach

- Suffix endings **-ing**, **-ed**, **-er**, **-est**, **-en**, **-able**, **-ish**, **-y**, **-ive**, **-ly**, **-ty**, **-less**, **-ness**, **-ment**, **-ful**

- Reading and spelling words with suffixes added to unchanging basewords

Additional Materials Needed

- 6.1 yellow Suffix Cards, Syllable Cards 3-6

- 6.1 Word Cards, Step 6 Student Reader and Student Rules Notebook

- Student Workbook 6A & 6B (optional)

- **Supplemental materials for B Level students**: Stories for Students, Travels with Ted

PART 1

Follow the procedure for Part 1.

PART 2

Put the Suffix Cards in two columns to distinguish between vowel and consonant suffixes. Students will need to distinguish between vowel and consonants for future Spelling Rules, so emphasize the two kinds. Endings can be added to a baseword to make longer words. Demonstrate with the word **bug** on the table. Add **s** to form **bugs**. **Bug** is the baseword and **s** is added to it - **s** is a **suffix**. A suffix is an ending that can be added to a baseword. There are two kinds: **vowel** suffixes begin with vowels and **consonant** suffixes begin with consonants. Make the word **quick** with cards. Add **-er**, **-est**, **-ly** and explain that different suffixes can be added to words.

Point out that the suffix -**ful** has one **l**, and the word **full** has two. Also, note that the suffix -**able**, contains an unstressed first syllable, /ə/; the word **able**, on the other hand, is accented on the first syllable, spoken /ā bl/. Teach that **y** as a suffix always says /ē/ and that -**less** and -**ness** each have a "bonus" **s**.

Make words and add suffixes. You can write basewords on index cards, but be sure the suffix addition doesn't alter the baseword's spelling or pronunciation. Students read the baseword first, and then the whole word including the suffix (**quickly** is read: **quick**, **quickly**).

Notebook Entry

(Spelling Rules Section) Review the definition of a baseword and a suffix, plus add examples of 6.1 suffixes to the appropriate page.

PART 3

Follow the procedure for Part 3.

PART 4

Students should read the wordlists by naming the baseword first and then the whole word. For example: **refine** / **refinement**; **filth** / **filthy**.

PART 5 **PART 6** Follow the procedures for Parts 5 and 6.

PART 7 Use blank Syllable Cards to represent the syllables in a baseword. Have students arrange the Suffix Cards in two columns: suffixes beginning with a vowel and suffixes beginning with a consonant.

Dictate the word **hopeful** and have students name the baseword (**hope**). One blank card will represent this baseword since it is monosyllabic. Now students pull down the Suffix Card -**ful**. The word must be spelled orally, while the students point to the cards. Continue dictating 6.1 words and have the students follows these procedures.

PART 8 For Spelling, the student must spell the baseword first. When **publisher** is dictated, the student must first name the baseword, publish, spell by syllables, **pub lish**, and then add the suffix.

PART 9 **PART 10** Follow the procedures for Parts 9 and 10.

 Notes / FYI
Suffixes taught thus far are all common Anglo-Saxon suffixes. The suffix -**able** is a Latin suffix.

Sometimes a suffix conveys meaning (**hopeless** vs. **hopeful**). Most often the suffix effects the part of speech (**depending** vs. **dependable**). These concepts may be presented during vocabulary discussion.

Weave with Questions
After suffixes have been taught, ask students to 'brainstorm' all the vowel suffixes and then, all the consonant suffixes they can remember. Place the corresponding Suffix Cards into columns as the students name them. Reread cards.

Have the student circle suffixes on wordlist, sentence and story pages.

After a student spells a word or sentence, have him underline the baseword (in syllables) and circle the suffix. **hope(ful)**

Ask, "What is the baseword?" and "What is the suffix?"

6.2 What to Teach

- Suffix ending -**ed** with the sounds /**d**/ and /**t**/.

- Reading and spelling words with suffix -**ed** added to unchanging basewords

Additional Materials Needed
- 6.2 Word Cards

PART 1

Students learn that the suffix -**ed** has three different sounds. It says /**ĕd**/ as in **responded** (as taught in Step 3.5), it says /**t**/ as in **dunked**, and it says /**d**/ as in **freshened**.

Notebook Entry
(Sound Section) Add /**d**/ and /**t**/ spelling options to the Sound Option Page.

PART 2

Tell students that this suffix means the past tense. Something already happened. For example, ask a student to stand up. Write **jump** on the board and tell the student to do it. Add the -**ed** Suffix Card and say, "You **jumped**." Have the student say "**jump** - **jumped**" and listen to the -**ed** sound /**t**/. Explain that -**ed** can be sounds /**ĕd**/, /**t**/ or /**d**/. Make examples of each, using the -**ed** Suffix Card.

Usually, students can "feel" when to read the sounds /**ed**/, /**t**/ or /**d**/ at the end of words. If a student can't do this, let him try all three sounds until he gets the correct one. It is too much memorization for a student to remember which letters demand a particular sound.

PART 3

A nice activity to classify words: Make three -**ed** index cards [-ed = /ed/] [-ed = /d/] [-ed = /t/]. Put these three index cards on a table and use 6.2 Word Cards (make additional examples) and have students classify words into the correct pile. For example, the index card with the word **jumped** would go in the -**ed** = /**t**/ category.

PART 4
PART 5

Follow the procedures for Parts 4 and 5.

PART 6

Ask, "What says /**d**/?" (-**d**, -**ed**) and "What says /**t**/?" (-**t**, -**ed**). See the "What Says?" page for Step 6 in the Dictation Book 1-6.

PART 7

Past tense meaning of -**ed** should be re-discussed. Students should understand that if they hear a word that means something is past, and it ends with the sound /**t**/ or /**d**/, it will be spelled with -**ed**. Do the following oral exercise. Say the entire word "**jumped**." Have the student repeat the word and then say the baseword. Do a few examples orally. Dictate words. Follow the same procedure used in Step 6.1 - Part 7, to practice spelling 6.2 words. Use index cards and the -**ed** Suffix Card.

PART 8
PART 9
PART 10

Follow the procedures for Parts 8, 9, and 10.

Weave with Questions
Instruct the student to circle the -**ed** suffixes on a wordlist. Then, have him indicate the sound by writing **ed**, **d** or **t** above the suffix (**clench e̊d**). Ask, "What sound do you hear for the -**ed** suffix?"

6.3   What to Teach

- Two suffixes can be added to a word

- Reading and spelling words with two suffixes added to unchanging basewords

Additional Materials Needed

- 6.3 Word Cards

PART 1

Follow the procedure for Part 1.

PART 2

Tell students that basewords can sometimes have two suffixes added to them. Make the word **hope** and add the Suffix Card -**ful** and the Suffix Card -**ly**. Tell students that two suffixes can be added to some basewords. Point out that now there are two **l**'s because the two suffixes each retain their spellings (-**ful** and -**ly**). Make several examples. Students should read the baseword *first*, then the entire word with baseword and suffixes (**hopefully** should be read: **hope** / **hopefully**).

PART 3

With a Word Card such as **hopelessly**, find the baseword and then have students identify the two suffixes -**less** and -**ly**. Tell the students that although these words are long, they are quite easy.

PART 4

The student should read the wordlist by naming the baseword first, then the entire word. For example: **effect** / **effectively**

PART 5

PART 6

Follow the procedures for Parts 5 and 6.

PART 7

For spelling preparation, follow the Step 6.1 procedures.

PART 8

Again, **be sure** the student names and spells the baseword and **then** adds the suffix.

PART 9

PART 10

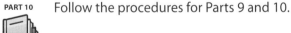

Follow the procedures for Parts 9 and 10.

Weave with Questions

Students should circle the two suffixes separately:

6.4   What to Teach

- New syllable type: Consonant-le

- Reading and spelling words with the consonant-le syllable

- The consonant-le syllable exception

Additional Materials Needed

- 6.4 Word Cards, 6.4 Syllable Cards

- Green **stle** Sound Card, white index cards

PART 1   Follow the procedure for Part 1.

PART 2   It's time to teach a new syllable type: consonant-le. Use the Sound Cards to review open, closed, and vowel-consonant-e syllables. Place cards on the table to form each syllable type. For example:

Discuss these syllables. Review them, using the student's Rules Notebook.

Tell your student that the fourth syllable is unusual. It can only be the last syllable in a multisyllabic word and it always has three letters. Two of the letters are always the same. Display the **l** and **e** Sound Cards. Tell the student that this syllable always has an **le** at the end. Now put a g in front of the l. Cover the **e** and ask the student to read the blend **gl**. Tell him that the **e** is silent - *again* the **e** volunteered! It is here because every syllable needs a vowel in it, so it just sits there, being the vowel. The **e** is silent and there is no vowel sound. The only letter that can change is the consonant before the **le**. Add various consonants to form: **ple, zle, tle, fle, ble, dle,** and **kle**. Each time, read the consonant and **l** together (**ple** = **pl**), etc. Then remind the student that this syllable is always at the end of a word. Add **ma** in front of **ple** to form **maple**. Pull the two syllables apart: **ma ple**.

Remind the student that the first syllable is open. If the vowel had a short sound it would need to be closed in. Change cards to form **aple**; then divide into two parts: **a ple**.

Tell him that in the word **apple**, you need another **p** to close in the **a** and make it short. Make another **p** on a white index card and add it to form **apple**. Provide more examples and have the student divide and read these words. They will always divide just before the consonant-le syllable.

In subsequent lessons, after the student has mastered the consonant-le words, remind the student that every syllable type has an exception. The consonant-le exception involves the letter combination **stle**. Use the green **stle** Sound Card to demonstrate. Whenever a word ends in **stle**, both the **t** and the **e** are silent. The **l** is the only letter sounded in the syllable; the **s** is considered part of the previous syllable. For example: **căs t̸l̸e̸**

Notebook Entry

(Syllable Section) The student must enter the consonant-le syllable into his notebook on a new page. Add the **stle** exception only after it is taught. Add the 6.4 syllable division rules to the Rules of Syllable Division page.

       Follow the procedures for Parts 3, 4, 5, and 6.

PART 3 PART 4 PART 5 PART 6

 PART 7 For spelling preparation, use the Sound Cards. Dictate a 6.4 word such as **bubble**. The student should repeat the word, saying one syllable at a time. Use the Sound Cards to spell the word. A blank ivory card can be used for the second letter **b** or the student can make a **b** on a white index card. Have the students name each syllable: **bub ble**, then spell each one. Remind the student that the **e** is silent, but needed! Point out that two **b**'s are needed to get the short vowel sound. Practice with several 6.4 words.

      Follow the procedures for Parts 8, 9, and 10.

PART 8 PART 9 PART 10

 Notes / FYI

Some other programs (and some dictionaries) add a schwa sound in the consonant-le syllable. The word **table** would be read **ta bəl**. This makes things more complicated for spelling. We therefore do not teach them to say a schwa sound in the consonant-le syllable. To simplify, read the consonant and **l** as a blend (**ta bl**). This works for decoding and helps eliminate confusion for spelling. Be sure the student doesn't read **ful** for **fl**, or **pul** for **pl**, etc. Make no vowel sound in this syllable.

There are words that sound like a consonant-le syllable that do have a schwa sound in the second syllable. These can be treated as sight words and added to the sight word Dictionary as needed (ex. **label**). The suffix -**al** will be taught in Step 10. Words such as **radical** sound like consonant-le words. For now, the student does not have to determine the spelling of -**cle** or -**cal** until that suffix is learned in Step 10.

 Weave with Questions

The student should mark wordlists to indicate syllable types:

ri fle   **wig gle**   **whis tle**
o -le   c -le   c

Step 1-6 Review / Application

Steps 1-6 establish a very firm base. The students should be left with no doubt that there is a system to the English language. They should be very good at dividing words into syllables for reading and working one syllable at a time for spelling. They should quickly and clearly see when words have a suffix or suffixes added.

The "carry-over" to non-controlled text begins to take hold and the students feel the success. It is now critical for students to practice reading non-controlled text with a teacher who understands what they have learned in order to master and apply it.

Most students should not get beyond Step 6 in one year, unless the program is being used with high-level students for spelling purposes. Most students require 2-3 years to complete the Wilson Reading System. Steps 1-6 are much less complex than Steps 7-12. These steps set a necessary strong foundation for the upper steps. Be sure 1-6 is firm before continuing. At the end of Step 6, it is a good time to "rest and digest" a bit. Do shortened review lessons. Practice outside reading with "non-controlled" text. This must now be done more formally with the student. When an outside text is selected, be sure to consider the following:

- Length: keep it manageable; short passages are best at the beginning.
- Interest: select a story or subject of interest.
- Level of reading: select something written at an easier level for the student. High-interest, low-level vocabulary books are useful with older students.
- Size of print: the bigger, the better; large print for the visually impaired might work well.

The teacher should take turns with the student when reading non-controlled text. Quickly "feed" students any unknown words that contain untaught elements. The student needs to read with a pencil point and should be taught how to break down words, etc. when needed. The teacher needs to model fluency, inflection, etc. The student might reread a paragraph after it is modeled. Incorporate visualization and retelling as the student reads the non-controlled text.

Step 7

At the end of this step, students should know:

- That **c** says /**s**/ when followed by **e**, **i**, and **y**
- That **g** usually says /**j**/ when followed by **e**, **i**, and **y**
- That silent **e** can be in a word simply to change the sound of **g** and **c**
- That no English word ends in **j**
- **dge** says /**j**/ and is used to end a word after short vowels and **tch** says /**ch**/ and is used after short vowels
- **ph** is a digraph and it says /**f**/
- **tion** says /**shŭn**/ and **sion** says /**shŭn**/ and /**zhŭn**/
- **ssion** is used directly after short vowels
- How to use a dictionary and/or electronic spell checker for sound option spelling

The upper Steps 7 through 12 are more complex and the pace usually slows down. This program takes one to three years to complete with a student. Most students take three years.

Steps 7 through 9 concentrate on "sound options". There are two or more ways to represent some sounds. The sound option procedure for spelling work must now include use of a dictionary or an electronic spell checker. Students must learn to list the possible spelling options and circle their first choice. They must then check the dictionary (or spell checker) for the correct spelling.

Some students will become very good at identifying and using the correct option without checking which one is correct, while other students will have much difficulty. This can vary greatly.

Be sure that all students practice the procedure (even if the choice is correct) so that the skill of option spelling can be applied easily without assistance.

A student's success at identifying the correct option depends upon:

- His/her visual memory for words
- His/her exposure to the word
- His/her natural "sense" for what seems right

On the other hand, some students will always need to check which option is correct. The teacher should tell the student (as well as the parents and other teachers) that this is necessary and absolutely acceptable.

Throughout Steps 7 through 9, certain sound options are used in particular situations. In these cases, the student will learn these rules. For example, to determine the spelling of /**ch**/, **tch** is used immediately after a short vowel sound. It is essential to teach these rules with the manipulation of Sound Cards as opposed to teaching the rule simply with language and requiring its memorization.

From Step 7 onward, teachers must continue with the "outside reading" application of skills with the student. The oral and silent reading of non-controlled text is extremely critical and should be done for 30 minutes or more, three times per week (minimum).

7.1   What to Teach

- **c** says /**s**/ when followed by **e, i, y**

- **g** usually says /**j**/ when followed by **e, i, y**

- How to read words with **g** /**j**/ and **c** /**s**

- Procedure for spelling words with spelling options /**j**/ and /**s**/

Additional Materials Needed
- 7.1 Word Cards, 7.1 Syllable Cards

- Step 7 Student Reader and Student Rules Notebook

- Student Workbook 7A (optional)

 PART 1   In the initial lesson, skip to Part 2. After teaching Part 2, present the ⌐c⌐ Sound Card and teach the student to say, "**c** - /**k**/ and **c** - /**s**/ when followed by **e, i,** and **y**." Likewise, present the **g** card and teach the student to respond, "**g** - /**g**/ and **g** - /**j**/ when followed by **e, i,** and **y**."

Notebook Entry
(Sound Section) Add **g** - /**j**/ and **c** - /**s**/

 PART 2   Tell the student that in Steps 7 through 12, he will learn that some letters have more than one sound. Teach that there is more than one way to represent many sounds. These are called **sound options**. Show the letter **s** and ask the student to name its sounds (/**s**/ and /**z**/). Then ask, "What else says /**z**/?" This is a sound option he already knows. Tell him that he must learn other options for sounds in our language. It can be confusing, yet these options are what make English so versatile. Explain that sound options occur because English developed from several languages.

Explain that **c** and **g** followed by **e, i** and **y** change their sounds. Use the **c** and **g** Sound Cards with the vowel cards to demonstrate.

Use Sound Cards to form the nonsense syllable ⌐c⌐⌐a⌐. Ask the student to tell you what sound that **c** makes in that syllable (/**k**/). Change the vowel to **e, i, o** and then **u**. Each time tell the student the sound of the **c**. Do the same with **g, a** etc. You can also make words and nonsense closed syllables for the student to read. Use Syllable Cards to make examples of multisyllabic words.

    to   to

 PART 3   **PART 4**   **PART 5**   Follow the procedures for Parts 3, 4, and 5.

 PART 6   Have the student spread out consonant cards in alphabetical order (see Substep 1.3). Ask "What says /**s**/?" (Student should select **s** and **c**.) Have him put the vowel cards **e, i,** and **y** after the **c** to demonstrate when it will say /**s**/:

Also ask, "What says /**j**/?"

PART 7

Dictate the 7.1 word **cinch**.

Have the student select the blank consonant card for the /**s**/ sound: [ ] [i] [n] [ch]

Ask the student, "What says /**s**/?" (**c** and **s**). Cover the blank card with **c** and then the **s**:

[c] [i] [n] [ch]   then   [s] [i] [n] [ch]

Tell him that only one option is correct. Ask him which option he believes is correct. Teach him how to use the spell checker or dictionary to determine the correct option. Dictate 7.1 words with /**j**/ and /**s**/. Have the student use the blank card and the dictionary or spell checker. Also dictate words from previous steps with /**j**/ spelled with **j** and /**s**/ spelled with **s**. For example, for the word **centrum**, the student can put out two Syllable Cards with the blank consonant card on the first syllable:

PART 8   **PART 9**   **PART 10**   Follow the procedures for Parts 8, 9, and 10.

Notes / FYI

Do not rush this Substep. You are setting the groundwork for more complex reading/spelling skills.

Spend time teaching Dictionary Skills. Have the student master alphabetical order with the placing of the Sound Cards on the table in four quadrants (see 1.3 in this manual). Divide the Dictionary into four quadrants (you can use a paper clip to separate sections). Initially, simply have the student locate the first letter of the given word. You then show him how to go to the next letter in the word, etc. Do this until the student is able to locate the words independently.

Weave with Questions

"What sound does the **c** (or **g**) make in this word?"
"What three vowels change the sounds of **c** and **g**?"

7.2   What to Teach

- How to read and spell words with a vowel-consonant-**g** or **c**, followed by **e**

- The sound **dge** - /**j**/

- How to read and spell words with **dge**

Additional Materials Needed

- 7.2 Word Cards, 7.2 Syllable Cards

- **dge** Sound Card

PART 1

In the first lesson, do not include the new sound **dge** in the quick drill. After Part 2, hold the [dge] card, say the letter-keyword-sound and have the student repeat, "**dge** - **fudge** - /**j**/." Include the **dge** card in the quick drill in subsequent lessons.

Notebook Entry

(Sound Section) The student must add **dge** - /**j**/

PART 2

Use Sound Cards to make the word **price**. Have the student read the word. Ask him to explain the two jobs of the silent **e** (it makes the vowel **i** long and it makes the **c** say /**s**/). Now add an **n** so that you form the word **prince**. Explain that **e** does not jump over two letters (**n** and **c**) so that the vowel **i** is not long, it is short. The **e** is there for one job only. Ask the student to explain the job of **e** (to make the **c** say /**s**/). Take away the **e** and ask the student to read the nonsense word **princ** - /**prink**/. Add the **e** and reread the word **prince** - /**prins**/. Make the word **plunge** with the Sound Cards [p] [l] [u] [n] [g] [e]. Tell the student that **e** only has one job and ask him to explain (the **e** makes the **g** say /**j**/). Ask if the vowel will be long or short (short). Have the student read the word. Make additional words with **nce** and **nge** to practice.

Next ask the student to name a letter in the English language that 'refuses' to end words (**v**). Tell him that there is another letter that will never end a word. Use the Sound Cards to make **fuj**. Ask the student to decode this /**fŭj**/. Explain that the letter **j** will not end any words in English. Ask him to name the other letter that says /**j**/ - (**g**). Replace the **j** card with **g** to form [f] [u] [g]. Ask him what letter volunteers to make **g** say /**j**/ - (hard working **e**). Add **e** to make **fuge**. The **e** can do two jobs so that this word says /**fūj**/ instead of /**fŭj**/. Add the letter **d** to spell **fudge**. Now there are two letters between the **u** and the **e**. Explain that the **d** acts as a buffer to keep the sound of the vowel short. The **e** therefore only has one job - to make the **g** say /**j**/. Replace the three letters [d] [g] [e] with the one [dge] Sound Card and have the student read the word.

Make additional **dge** words using the [dge] card. Remind the student that the preceding vowel is always short.

Make the 7.2 words with Syllable Cards. Have the student decode. Discuss the sounds as appropriate.

PART 3   **PART 4**   **PART 5**   Follow the procedures for Parts 3, 4, and 5.

 PART 6 Spread out vowel and consonant cards, including **dge**. Ask, "What says /**j**/?" Have the student select **j**, **dge**, and **g**. Have him put the vowel cards **e**, **i** and **y** after the **g**. Ask him to point to the card that says /**j**/ after a short vowel at the end of a word (**dge**).

 PART 7 Dictate the word **dance**. Have the student repeat then find the letters to spell the word. If the student spells this word with the letters **dans**, ask him to find other letters to replace the **s**. Explain that the **s** makes it seem as though the word **dans** is a baseword plus suffix -**s**. Thus the word is spelled with **ce**. Dictate **nce**, **nge**, and **dge** words. Have the student find the letters to spell the words.

PART 8   **PART 9**   **PART 10**   Follow the procedures for Parts 8, 9, and 10.

 Weave with Questions
"Is the vowel long or short?"

"What is the job of **e** in this word?"

"What letters spell /**j**/ at the end of a word after a short vowel?"

"Will the letter **j** ever end an English word?"

7.3   What to Teach

- The sound of **tch** - /**ch**/ and **ph** - /**f**/

- How to read and spell words with **tch**

- How to read words with **ph** and use option spelling to determine the spelling of /**f**/.

Additional Materials Needed

- 7.3 Word Cards, 7.3 Syllable Cards

- **tch** and **ph** Sound Cards

 PART 1 In the first lesson, do not include **tch** and **ph** cards in the quick drill. After Part 2, present these two cards. Hold up the ⌜tch⌝ and have the student repeat **tch** - **catch** - /**ch**/. Hold up the ⌜ph⌝ card, say the letters-keyword-sound, and have the students repeat, "**ph** - **phone** - /**f**/." Include these cards in subsequent lessons.

Notebook Entry

(Sound Section) The student must add the sounds of **ph** and **tch** to the digraph page of his notebook.

 PART 2 Make the word **fudge**, using the ⌜dge⌝ card. Have the student read this word. Ask him to name the sound of **dge** (/**j**/). Tell him this is not a digraph because *di* means *two* and **dge** is three letters. The **dge** is called a **trigraph** since *tri* means *three*. The **dge** is three letters that make one sound. Ask the student after what kind of vowel (long or short) is this trigraph used (short). Tell the student that there is another trigraph. Display the **tch** card. Make the word **catch**. Tell the student that **tch** says /**ch**/. Have him read the word and ask him if the vowel is long or short (short). Explain that the **tch** is a trigraph and this trigraph is only used directly after a short vowel. Make additional **tch** words and have the student decode them.

Next, tell the student that there is one other digraph to learn. Have him name as many digraphs as possible. As he names them, place the cards on the table or magnetic board (**sh**, **ck**, **ch**, **th**, **wh**). Present the **ph** card and tell the student that it says /**f**/. Make the word **phone** with Sound Cards. Have the student read this word and review the sound of **ph**. Make additional **ph** words.

 PART 3   **PART 4**   **PART 5** Follow the procedures for Parts 3, 4, and 5.

 PART 6 Ask, "What says /**ch**/?" (**ch** and **tch**). Have the student find these cards. Ask which one is used after a short vowel (**tch**). Also ask, "What says /**f**/?" (**f** and **ph**). Have the student find these cards.

PART 7 Dictate words with the sound of /**ch**/. Include both **tch** words and **ch** words. Have the student make the words with the Sound Cards. Be sure to reinforce that in words with a short vowel immediately before /**ch**/, the sound of /**ch**/ must be spelled with **tch**. Point to the short vowel in a word such as **pitch**. Ask, "Is the sound of the vowel long or short?" (short). "How do you spell /**ch**/ after a short vowel?" (**tch**).

Additionally, you can also simply practice the selection of **ch** or **tch**. Put ⌐ch⌐ and ⌐tch⌐ Sound Cards on the table. Say a word with the /**ch**/ sound. Have the student select the correct spelling of /**ch**/: **tch** or **ch** and give the explanation for his choice. Some words to use for this activity include: **inch**, **patch**, **chap**, **finch**, **chestnut**, **stitch**, and **enchant**. Dictate the word **phone**. Have the student use a blank ivory card to represent the sound of /**f**/ (⌐ ⌐o⌐n⌐e⌐). Next ask him to find the two options for /**f**/ and **ph**. Use the dictionary or a spell checker to determine the spelling of the sound /**f**/.

Explain that words with the sound /**f**/ can be spelled either with an **f** or **ph** but the **f** is much more common. The student should use a dictionary or spell checker to determine the correct spelling. Dictate additional words with the sound of /**f**/.

Note: Advanced students can be told to use the **ph** for scientific words. Explain that words with **ph** are Greek in origin.

Notebook Entry
(Spelling Section) The student should add the **dge** spelling option and the **tch** spelling generalization to the spelling section of his notebook.

PART 8 **PART 9** **PART 10** Follow the procedures for Parts 8, 9, and 10.

 Notes / FYI
Words such as **rich**, **which**, **such** and **much** do not follow the **tch** spelling rule. If students have difficulty spelling these words, add them to their sight word dictionary.

 Weave with Questions
"What says /**f**/ in this word?"

"When do you use **tch**?"

"What says /**ch**/ in this word?"

"What letters in this word are a trigraph?"

7.4 What to Teach

- The sounds of **tion** - /**shŭn**/ and **sion** - /**shŭn**/ and /**zhŭn**/

- How to read and spell words with **tion** and **sion**

- How to use spelling options for words with /**shŭn**/

- How to spell words with /**zhŭn**/

Additional Materials Needed

- 7.4 Word Cards, 7.4 Syllable Cards

- **tion** and **sion** Sound Card

 PART 1

In the first lesson, do not include the new sounds **tion** and **sion** in the quick drill. After Part 2, hold the **sion** card, say the letters-keyword-sound and have the student repeat, "**sion** - **mansion** - /**shŭn**/, **sion** - **television** - /**zhŭn**/." Hold the **tion** card and say the letter name-keyword-sounds and have the student repeat "**tion** - **vacation** - /**shŭn**/".

Include the sion and tion cards in subsequent lessons.

Notebook Entry

(Sound Section) The student must add the sounds of **tion** and **sion**.

 PART 2

Put the **tion** and **sion** cards on the table or magnetic board. Tell the student that these cards both say /**shŭn**/. Use the Syllable Cards to display the words: | man | sion | and | va | ca | tion |. Have students decode these words.

Explain that the **sion** can also say /**zhŭn**/ as in **television**. Make words with /**zhŭn**/ and have the students decode them.

Advanced Students

Use Sound Cards to make the word **mission**. Divide the word into syllables, with the cards | mis | sion |. Explain that the **s** in the first syllable closes in the vowel to make it short, but the **s** is silent. Cover the **s** and read **mĭ** /**shŭn**/. Tell the student that in words with **ssion**, the vowel before the **s** is short, and the **s** is silent. Make additional **ssion** words to practice.

PART 3 **PART 4** **PART 5**

      Follow the procedures for Parts 3, 4, and 5.

 PART 6

Display the sion and tion cards along with other cards. Ask, "What says /**shŭn**/?" Have the student find the **sion** and **tion** cards. Ask, "What says /**zhŭn**/?" Have the student find the **sion** card.

PART 7 Use 7.4 Syllable Cards to dictate /**shŭn**/ and /**zhŭn**/ words. Turn Syllable Cards face down. Dictate a word and have the student spell the word one syllable at a time. The student should use a spell checker to determine the spelling of /**shŭn**/ as needed. Make additional words using index cards.

PART 8 **PART 9** **PART 10** Follow the procedures for Parts 8, 9, and 10.

Notes / FYI

The endings **sion** and **tion** are actually noun-forming suffixes:

collide - collision

divide - division

inject - injection

digest - digestion

Since these suffixes are added to basewords and roots in unusual ways, it is complicated to teach them as suffixes. This strategy may be explained to advanced students. It can be helpful in determining the spelling **sion** and **tion**. Words ending in /**t**/, for example, take the **tion** spelling (**isolate**, **isolation**, etc.) The **tion** option should be selected after a long vowel (**vacā -tion**, **solü -tion**). The **ssion** should be selected after a short vowel (except /**ĭ**/). After /**ĭ**/ select **tion** unless the word is **mission** (**mĭssion**, **concŭssion**, **ignĭtion**).

Weave with Questions

"What letters say /**shŭn**/ in this word?"

"What letters say /**zhŭn**/ in this word?"

In words with **ssion**: "What letter is there to close in the vowel, but is silent?"

7.5   What to Teach

- How to read contractions

- How to form and spell contractions

Additional Materials Needed

- 7.5 Word Cards

- Index cards to make sight Word Cards:

| does | would | could | should | you | do | who | they | are | what |

- An index card with an **apostrophe**: `'`

PART 1   No new sounds are taught.

PART 2   Present the Sight Word Cards listed above. Have the student read these cards. If the student is unable to read any of the cards, teach the student using the method to teach sight words. See "Sight Word Instruction" in the Introduction of this Manual. Do not proceed until the student is able to read the words quickly.

When the sight words can be read easily, put the sight Word Card `does` on the table or magnetic board. Use the Sound Cards to make the word **not** `n` `o` `t`. Have the student read the words **does not**. Replace the **o** in the word **not** with the apostrophe card `n` `'` `t`. Explain that this word is now **doesn't**. Tell the student that sometimes it sounds better to put these two words together. It is easier and quicker to say it when it is shortened. Use **does not** then **doesn't** in a sentence. Explain that the **o** is replaced with an apostrophe and there is no vowel sound: **n't** = (**nt**). Make **should**, **could** and **would** with **not**. Replace the **o** in **not** with an apostrophe and have the student read these words. Do other words with **not**. Show that in the words **can not**, the apostrophe replaces the **n** and the **o**.

Next, do the same with the other contractions. Replace Sound Card(s) with the apostrophe and have the student read the contraction.

PART 3   Be sure to make Word Cards with additional contractions since the WRS Word Cards merely provide a sample.

PART 4   Prior to presenting wordlists to the student, be sure the contractions on a given list were practiced in Parts 2 and 3.

PART 5   **PART 6**   Follow the procedures for Parts 5 and 6.

PART 7 Dictate the sight words listed at the beginning of this section. Have the student spell these words. If the student is unable to spell any of these words, teach the student using the method to teach sight words (see the Sight Word Instruction in the Introduction of this Manual). Continue to review the spelling of these sight words in subsequent lessons until the student securely knows the spelling of these words before proceeding.

When the sight words can be easily spelled, teach the formation of contractions. Spread out the Sound Cards (not the green welded sounds). Also put out a blank index card and the index card with the apostrophe.

Dictate the words **does not**. Have the student put a blank index card for the sight word **does** and find the Sound Cards for the word **not**: ☐ n o t

Have him spell **does** (**d** - **o** - **e** - **s**), **not** (**n** - **o** - **t**). Next say the word **doesn't** and have him repeat. Ask him to replace the silent letter in the word **not** with the apostrophe card. Lastly, spell the whole word **doesn't**. Dictate other contractions. Have the student spell the word with the index card, Sound Cards, and apostrophe.

PART 8   **PART 9**   **PART 10**   Follow the procedures for Parts 8, 9, and 10.

Helpful Hints / Activities

Make strips for the student to practice reading:

what is	=	what's
that is	=	that's

and

that's	=	that is
what's	=	what is

Weave with Questions

"What two words does the contraction stand for?"
"What letters are missing in this contraction?"

Step 8

At the end of this step, students should know:

- The r-controlled syllable type
- The sounds for **ar**, **or**, **er**, **ir**, and **ur**
- How to use sound option spelling principles for /ər/
- When **r** is doubled after a vowel, the vowel is often short
- **or** and **ar** in an unstressed final syllable say /ər/
- How to read and spell words with **ard**, **ward**, **para**

This step introduces the fifth type of syllable found in English words: The r-controlled syllable. Although words with these sounds (**ar**, **er**, **ir**, **or**, **ur**) are sometimes easy to read, students must apply sound option principles for spelling. For this reason, this syllable type is taught in the second half of the program, rather than in the first six steps.

Continue to practice the spelling option work with the dictionary or spell checker. The student should become independent at determining the correct spelling when dictated a word with a spelling option (such as the /ər/ sound).

Remember to do non-controlled reading in addition to the controlled reading. You should tell the student any unknown word if it contains word structure not yet taught.

8.1   What to Teach

- New type of syllable: r-controlled

- Sounds: **ar**, **er**, **ir**, **or**, **ur**

- How to read words with r-controlled syllables

- How to spell words with r-controlled syllables using sound option spelling

Additional Materials Needed

- Sound Cards: **ar**, **er**, **ir**, **or**, **ur**

- 8.1 Word Cards

- Step 8 Student Reader and Student Rules Notebook

- Student Workbook 8A (optional)

PART 1

Spread out **ar**, **er**, **ir**, **or** and **ur** Sound Cards. Ask the student what these cards have in common (the letter **r**). Tell them that the **r** "controls" the vowel sound. The vowel is not long or short - it is controlled by the **r**. Teach the keyword for each sound.

Notebook Entry

(Sound Section) Students must add r-controlled vowel page.

PART 2

Tell the student that whenever a syllable has an r-controlled sound in it, the syllable is called an r-controlled syllable. Make the word b ar k. Tell the student this is an r-controlled syllable because it has **ar**. Review the other kinds of syllables learned thus far (closed, v-e, open, -le). The r-controlled is the fifth kind of syllable found in English words. Make r-controlled (8.1) words on the table with the Sound Cards. The student can tap these words as well, if needed. The r-controlled sounds will get one tap.

 PART 3   **PART 4**   **PART 5**   Follow the procedures for Parts 3, 4, and 5.

PART 6

Use the "What Says?" page in the Dictation Book to select sounds. Be sure to display the new r-controlled sounds. Ask, "What says /ər/?" (**er**, **ir**, **ur**), "What says /**or**/" (**or**), and "What says /**ar**/?" (**ar**).

PART 7

Dictate r-controlled words. The student should repeat the word, tap it out, and locate the Sound Cards that correspond to each tap.

Tell the student that /**ar**/ and /**or**/ are clearly spelled. The /ər/ sound, however, can be spelled **er**, **ir**, **ur**. The **er** combination is most common. The student should use sound option spelling skills with these words. For example, dictate the word **lurk**. Have the student put a blank peach card on the /**er**/ sound l k, pull down the three options (**lerk**, **lirk**, **lurk**), choose one and check its spelling in the dictionary or with an electronic spell checker.

Notebook Entry

(Sound Section) Students should start /ər/ spelling option chart.

Follow the procedures for Parts 8, 9, and 10.

 Weave with Questions

"Is this syllable r-controlled?"

"What does that tell you?"

"What three vowel-r combinations sound alike?"

Teach students to mark these syllables:

ba(r)k   **b(ir)d**
   r   r

Notebook Entry

(Syllable Section) Students must add the description of r-controlled syllables and examples.

 Helpful Hints / Activities

This activity helps to review syllable types and emphasizes the differences. Give the student a paper divided into five columns, with syllable names at the top of each:

closed	v-e	open	-le	r-controlled
clap	**flame**	**shy**	**rifle**	**burn**
blimp	**stove**	**flu**	**rumble**	**farm**
stem	**bride**	**she**	**marble**	**dirt**

Dictate one-syllable words, two-syllable for consonant-le words. Have the student spell the word in the correct column and mark the vowels. If a word ends in consonant-le, it goes in that column, but both syllables are marked.

 Notes / FYI

Treat words with a vowel, an **r**, and an **e** (**spare**, **fire**) as v-e rather than r-controlled. Tell students the **e** "wins out" since it is stronger due to all the work it does.

8.2 What to Teach

· Combining r-controlled syllable (**ar** and **or**) with other syllables to form multisyllabic words

Additional Materials Needed

· 8.2 Word Cards

· 8.2 Syllable Cards

 PART 1

No new sounds are taught. Be sure to include all r-controlled vowels taught in 8.1.

 PART 2

Use Sound Cards to form the word f o r . Review r-controlled syllable. With Sound Cards, form the syllable **get**. Explain that an r-controlled syllable can combine with the four other types of syllables learned thus far. Demonstrate and discuss:

for get = r-controlled + closed

hard ware = r-controlled + vowel-consonant-e

re mark = open + r-controlled

mar ble = r-controlled + consonant-le

Explain that this Substep presents words that combine **or** and **ar** r-controlled syllables with other syllables. Use Syllable Cards to practice additional words.

 PART 3   **PART 4**   **PART 5**   **PART 6** Follow the procedures for Parts 3, 4, 5, and 6.

 PART 7

Use 8.2 Syllable Cards. Dictate the word. The student should repeat the word then name and spell one syllable at a time.

 PART 8   **PART 9**   **PART 10** Follow the procedures for Parts 8, 9, and 10.

 Helpful Hints / Activities

Make up several syllable matches with two-syllable words. Have the student match syllables to form real words. For example:

syllables		words
re	nish	remark
tar	get	tarnish
for	mark	forget
part	ment	partner
tor	ner	torment

8.3   What to Teach

- How to read multisyllabic words with /ər/

- How to spell multisyllabic words with /ər/ and use the spell checker or dictionary

Additional Materials Needed
- 8.3 Word Cards, 8.3 Syllable Cards

 PART 1

Follow the procedure for Part 1.

 PART 2

Spread out **er**, **ir**, and **ur** Sound Cards er   ir   ur . Ask the student to name the sound (/ər/). Make the word **sister**. Ask the student to divide it into syllables and read it. Explain that this Substep combines **er**, **ir**, and **ur** syllables with other syllables to form multisyllabic words. Make additional 8.3 words to demonstrate. Also, use 8.3 Syllable Cards to practice these words.

 PART 3   **PART 4**   **PART 5**   **PART 6**   Follow the procedures for Parts 3, 4, 5, and 6.

 PART 7

Spread out **er**, **ir**, and **ur** Sound Cards. Turn the Syllable Cards for the word **burlap** over so that they are face down. Dictate the word **burlap**. Have the student repeat the word (in syllables) as he points to blank Syllable Cards: ☐ ☐

Ask him to point to the syllable with the /ər/ sound. Then ask, "How can you spell /ər/?" (**er, ir, ur**). Have the student tell you the other letters in the word. Write them down, leaving a blank to represent /ər/: **b**☐**lap**. Insert the /ər/ cards to show the student each choice:

b er **lap**   **b** ir **lap**   **b** ur **lap**

Have him select one of these vowel cards. The student should then check his choice with a dictionary or spell checker. Turn over the **bur** **lap** Syllable Cards when the correct choice is identified. Have the student name and spell the word (one syllable at a time). Use blank index cards to practice additional 8.3 words.

 PART 8   **PART 9**   **PART 10**   Follow the procedures for Parts 8, 9, and 10.

 Notes / FYI

Two-syllable words with a closed syllable + **er** double the consonant to help maintain short sound (**hammer**, **suffer**, **supper**, **zipper**, etc.). These are similar to "bunny rabbit" words. However, the letter **v** never doubles (**never**, **river**, **sliver**, etc.).

 Weave with Questions

"What says /ər/?"

8.4   What to Teach

- Exception to r-controlled syllable
- How to read and spell words with **rr**

Additional Materials Needed

- 8.4 Word Cards, 8.4 Syllable Cards
- Make an additional **r** consonant card: `r`

PART 1

Follow the procedure for Part 1.

PART 2

Use Sound Cards to make the word `c` `ar`. Have the student read the word. Ask him the sound for **ar** (/**ar**/). Tell the student that the r-controlled syllable has exceptions too. Put an **r** consonant card and the vowel **y** card with **car**: `c` `ar` `r` `y`. Tell the student that this word has two **r**'s (point to them). Replace the **ar** card with the **a** vowel card and the extra **r**: `c` `a` `r` `r` `y`

Tell the student that the double **r** usually changes the preceding vowel to a short sound. Point to the **a** and ask the student to give the short sound of **a** (/**ă**/). Read the word **carry** and have the student listen to the short vowel. Explain that the double **r** makes the vowel short. Make other 8.4 words with the individual vowel card followed by two **r**'s to practice. Spread out vowel cards and the two **r** consonant cards. Ask the student, "What says /**ă**/?" He should point to the **a**. Put one **r** after **a**: `a` `r`. Ask the student if the **a** says /**ă**/ now (no). Add another **r**: `a` `r` `r`. Ask the same question and this time the answer should be "Yes."

Notebook Entry

(Syllable Section) Add the **rr** exception to the r-controlled syllable.

Advanced Students

Write **para** on an index card. Tell the student that **para** is a prefix. Explain that it can be added to the beginning of another word part (a root). Read it to the student (/**păr ə**/). Make words with the `para` card and Sound Cards.

Next make the word `a` `r` `i` `s` `e` with Sound Cards. Divide it into syllables. Have the student read the word. Ask, "What does **a** say?" (/**ŭ**/). Remind the student that **a** says /**ŭ**/ in an open syllable exception. Next make the word **arid**. Point out the letters **a, r, i**. Read the word to the student and ask him the sound of **a** (/**ă**/). Tell him that in words with **ar** then another vowel, often the first vowel is short. It may say /**ŭ**/ or /**ă**/. Make additional examples to practice.

Notebook Entry

(Syllable Selection) Add the **para** and a-r-vowel exceptions to the r-controlled syllable.

Follow the procedures for Parts 3, 4, 5, and 6.

PART 3 bat **PART 4** **PART 5** **PART 6**

 PART 7 Spread out r-controlled vowel cards, individual vowel cards and consonant cards. Dictate an 8.4 word such as **hurry**. Have the student repeat the word. Ask him, "Do you hear a short vowel before the **r** sound?" (yes). Ask him how many **r**'s he will need after the vowel to make it short (two). Have him make the word with the Sound Cards:

Intersperse r-controlled with r-controlled exceptions. The student should use the r-controlled cards (**ar**, **er**, **ir**, **or**, **ur**) if the syllable has an r-controlled sound, and individual vowel cards followed by two **r**'s if the vowel has a short sound.

Advanced Students
After you teach about **para** and a-r-vowel, dictate **para** and a-r-vowel words. Have the student use the Sound Cards to practice spelling these words.

   Follow the procedures for Parts 8, 9, and 10.

PART 8 **PART 9** **PART 10**

 Notes / FYI
Teach the student how to mark these words as exceptions:

hŭr rȳ
 ✗   o

8.5　What to Teach

- The sound of **ar** and **or** at the end of multisyllabic words

- How to read and spell words with **ar** and **or** at the end of multisyllabic words

- How to read and spell words with the ending **ard** and the suffix -**ward**

Additional Materials Needed

- 8.5 Word Cards, 8.5 Syllable Cards

- **w a r d** Suffix Card

PART 1

In the initial lesson, proceed to Part 2. In subsequent lessons, the student must give both sounds for **ar** and **or**. Be sure they give the /ər/ sound when presented with **ar** and **or** cards. Teach keywords.

Notebook Entry

(Sound Section) Add the keywords **doctor** and **beggar** to the **or** and **ar** sounds. Also add these two options to the /ər/ option list.

PART 2

Spread out r-controlled Sound Cards. Have the student give sounds. Ask him to separate the three cards that say /ər/:

Tell the students that the **ar** and **or** can also say /ər/. Use the Syllable Cards to make the words **solar** and **doctor**. Tell the students that **ar** and **or** say /ər/ at the end of multisyllabic words. Point to the **ar** and **or** and ask them to repeat the sound /ər/ after you. Now have them decode the words with the /ər/ sound. Practice additional 8.5 words with **ar** and **or** at the end.

When the student has mastered **ar** and **or** at the end of words, make the word **backward** using the **w a r d** Suffix Card. Tell the student that **ward** is a suffix. Next use the Sound Cards to make the word **wizard**. Explain that the letters **ard** say /ərd/ when unstressed at the end of a multisyllabic word. Make additional **ard** words for the student to decode.

Notebook Entry

(Syllable Section) The student should add the **or**, **ar**, **ard**, and **ward** exceptions to the r-controlled syllable.

PART 3

PART 4

PART 5

Follow the procedures for Parts 3, 4, and 5.

PART 6

Spread out r-controlled cards. Ask, "What says /ər/?" (**er**, **ir**, **ur**, and **or** and **ar** at the end of multisyllabic words).

Use 8.5 Syllable Cards or blank Syllable Cards. If using 8.5 Syllable Cards, turn them over so that the blank side is face up. (Be sure to only use words with **ar** and **or** at the end until **ward** and **ard** are also taught.)

Ask the student, "What says /ər/?" (**ar**, **or**, **er**, **ir**, **ur**). Ask which two say /ər/ only at the end of a multisyllabic word (**ar** and **or**). Put those two cards under the second blank Syllable Card:

Ask the student, "What is the most common spelling of the /ər/ sound?" (**er**). Add that card under the second syllable. Tell the student that multisyllabic words end in **er**, **ar**, or **or**. Remove the **ir** and **ur** cards. Tell him that these two options do not end multisyllabic words. Dictate 8.5 words. Use sound option spelling to determine the correct ending **er**, **ar**, or **or**. Include **er** words such as **singer**, **thriller**, **jumper**, **fender**, and **drinker**.

PART 8   **PART 9**   **PART 10**   Follow the procedures for Parts 8, 9, and 10.

Dictate words with the suffix -**ward**. Students should use the [**w a r d**] Suffix Card to spell these words. Also dictate words ending in **ard**. Students should name and spell one syllable at a time while pointing to blank Syllable Cards.

Notes / FYI

All multisyllabic words ending in /ər/ (**er**, **ar**, and **or**) can be *nouns*. The **er** choice is the most common.

If a word is an *adjective*, choose **er** if it is comparative (**strong** - **stronger** - **strongest**); otherwise choose **ar** (**muscular**, **regular**, **popular**).

If a word is a *verb*, choose **er** (**stutter**, **clatter**, **plunder**)

The above information can be taught to students only if they know the difference between nouns, verbs, and adjectives. Otherwise, wait until those parts of speech are known. In the meantime, treat the spelling of /ər/ at the end of words as sound options.

Step 9

At the end of this step, students should know:

- The vowel digraph/diphthong "D" syllable type
- The sounds for **ai**, **ay**, **ee**, **ey**, **oa**, **oe**, **ue**, **oi**, **oy**, **au**, **aw**, **ou**, **ow**, **oo**, **ea**, **eu**, **ew**, and **ui**
- How to read words with the above sounds
- How to use sound option spelling procedures to spell words with the above sounds

Students will learn the sixth and last type of syllable: the vowel digraph/diphthong "D" syllable. This syllable type contains either a vowel digraph or a diphthong. A vowel digraph is two letters that represent one vowel sound (**ee**). A diphthong is two or more letters that begin with one vowel sound and glide into another vowel sound (**oi**). The student does not need to learn the difference. It is important that he knows the letter combinations and the sound or sounds that the combination makes. These are gradually mastered with the help of keywords. These first vowel combinations also include those with more than one sound such as **ou**, **ow**, **oo**, and **ea**. The student must learn to be flexible when trying to decode these words. Throughout this step, be sure to continue work with the dictionary and/or electronic spell checker to determine spelling options.

9.1　What to Teach

- New type of syllable (vowel digraph/diphthong "D" syllable)
- Sounds: **ai** and **ay**
- How to read words with **ai** and **ay**
- How to use spelling option procedures to determine the spelling of /ā/ sounds

Additional Materials Needed

- Sound Cards **ay**, **ai**
- 9.1 Word Cards, 9.1 Syllable Cards
- Step 9 Student Reader and Student Rules Notebook
- Student Workbook 9A (optional)
- Make an extra **a** vowel card

 PART 1　Present the **ai** and **ay** Sound Cards. Tell the student that these two cards have letters that say the sound /ā/. Say letter names-keyword-sound and have the student repeat, "**ai** - **bait** - /ā/ and **ay** - **play** - /ā/."

Notebook Entry

(Sound Section) The student must add **ai** and **ay** to the new vowel combination page of his notebook.

 PART 2　Form the words **bait** and **play** using the Sound Cards. Have the student tap and read these words (each word gets three taps.) Explain that in Step 9, the student will learn the last type of syllable - the vowel digraph/diphthong "D" syllable. Tell the student that whenever there are two vowels together or double vowels, such as **ai** and **ay**, it is a vowel digraph or diphthong. Tell the student that he simply has to remember them as double vowels. A syllable with a double vowel is called a "D" syllable.

Make some **ai** and **ay** words. The student can tap these words as needed. The word **may** would be tapped /m/ - one tap, /ā/ - one tap. Use the Syllable Cards to make multisyllabic words. Have the student decode the words. Have the student identify the "D" syllable in multisyllabic words. The student can circle the **ai** and **ay** with his index finger to identify the double vowel.

PART 3　**PART 4**　**PART 5**　Follow the procedures for Parts 3, 4, and 5.

 PART 6　Spread out all peach vowel cards taught thus far. Also make an additional **a** vowel card (use a peach index card) and put out a blank consonant card. Ask, "What says /ā/?" The student should pull down the cards **a**, **ai**, **ay** and also **a** - blank - **e**. Be sure he says the letters in response to the question as he finds the cards. Review other sounds as well.

PART 7

Keep the **ai**, **ay**, **a**, and **a** - blank - **e** cards spread out. Explain that these are all spelling options for the sound of /**ā**/. Ask the student to identify which of these options ends an open syllable **a**. Explain that the most common spelling of the /**ā**/ sound when /**ā**/ ends a syllable is **a** (**va ca tion**, **ta ble**).

Tell the student that **ay** is most common at the end of words. Demonstrate some words such as **play** and **stay**. Next, make the words **plane** and **plain**. Have the student read these. Discuss the meaning of both words. Explain that both **ai** and **a-e** are used to spell the sound of /**ā**/ when a consonant sound follows the /**ā**/ sound in the syllable. Sometimes both spellings are used to create words with different meanings. A dictionary or spell checker must be used as needed to check the spelling.

Dictate words with /**ā**/, including **ai**, **ay**, **a-e**, and **a** spellings. Have the student select an option for the /**ā**/ sound and then use a spell checker or dictionary to confirm the choice.

Notebook Entry
(Sound Section) The student should begin the chart for spelling options for /**ā**/.

PART 8   **PART 9**   **PART 10**   Follow the procedures for Parts 8, 9, and 10.

Notes / FYI
Some vowel combinations are vowel digraphs (two vowels together making one sound). Other vowel combinations are diphthongs (letters that begin with one vowel sound and glide into another vowel sound). The **ai** and **ay** are actually vowel diphthong sounds. When making the /**ā**/ sound, notice how your mouth begins in one position and ends in another position. This information is helpful for you to know. For example, students might hear an additional sound in a word with /**ā**/ (such as the long /**ē**/ sound). This sometimes accounts for spelling errors such as **plaen** for **plane**. Most often, it is best to let the students call all vowel combinations, "double vowels" rather than worry about which are digraphs and which are diphthongs. The definitions can be explained and they can be added to the notebook; however, also explain that it is easier simply to identify the vowel combination and memorize the key-word.

Weave with Questions
"Find the double vowel in this word."

Teach students to mark this syllable type:

pl**ay**   dr**ai**n
  d   d

9.2 What to Teach

- Sounds: **ee** and **ey**

- How to read words with **ee** and **ey**

- How to use sound option spelling procedures to determine the spelling of /ē/ sounds

Additional Materials Needed

- Sound Cards **ee**, **ey**

- 9.2 Word Cards, 9.2 Syllable Cards

- Make two extra **e** vowel cards

PART 1

Present the **ee** and **ey** Sound Cards. Tell the student that these two cards have letters that say the sound /ē/. Say the letter names-keyword-sound and have the student repeat, "**ee** - **jeep** - /ē/ and **ey** - **valley** - /ē/."

Notebook Entry

(Sound Section) The student must add **ee** and **ey** to the vowel combination page of his notebook.

PART 2

Form the words **jeep** and **key** using the Sound Cards. Have the student tap and read these words (**jeep** = three taps, **key** = two taps). Tell him that these words have double vowels as well. Have him circle the double vowels with his index finger. Make some one-syllable words with Sound Cards. Have the student decode the words (tap as needed). Make multisyllabic words with Syllable Cards. The student can also identify the "D" syllable and circle the double vowel with his index finger. Reinforce the sounds with keywords.

PART 3

PART 4

PART 5

Follow the procedures for Parts 3, 4, and 5.

PART 6

Spread out all peach vowel cards taught thus far and a blank consonant card. Also make two additional **e** cards using a peach index card. Ask, "What says /ē/?" The student should pull down the cards, **e**, **e** - blank - **e**, **y**, **ee**, and **ey**. Be sure he says the letters as he finds the cards.

PART 7

Keep the /ē/ cards displayed. Explain that these are spelling options for the sound /ē/. Make the following words: **meet**, **candy**, and **donkey**. Ask the student to identify the word that has a consonant after the /ē/ sound in the syllable (**ee**). Explain that **ee** is the most common choice whenever the sound /ē/ is followed by a consonant. Make the word **Pete** and tell the student **e** - blank - **e** might also be used but it is uncommon. Isolate the words **candy** and **donkey**. Ask the student which word has the /ē/ sound spelled the way he learned first (**candy**). Tell him that **y** is the most common way to spell /ē/ at the end of multisyllabic words. Next tell him that **ee** and **e** can end one-syllable words and **e** usually ends open syllables within words (make the words **bee** and **be** and remark as you explain this). Dictate words with /ē/, including **e**, **e-e**, **y**, **ee** and **ey**. Have the student select an option for the /ē/ sound and then use a spell checker or dictionary to confirm the choice.

     Follow the procedures for Parts 8, 9, and 10.

Notebook Entry
(Sound Section) The student should add to the chart for spelling options for /ē/.

 Weave with Questions
"Can you find the double vowel in this word?"

Mark words with **ee** and **ey**:

9.3 What to Teach

- Sounds: **oa**, **oe** and **ue**
- How to read words with **oa**, **oe** and **ue**
- Sound option spelling procedures to determine the spelling of /ō/, /ū/ and /ü/.

Additional Materials Needed
- Sound Cards: **oa**, **oe**, **ue**
- 9.3 Word Cards, 9.3 Syllable Cards
- Use one extra **e** vowel card

PART 1 Present the **oa** and **oe** Sound Cards. Tell the student that these two cards have letters that say the sound /ō/. Say the letter names-keyword and sound and have the student repeat: **oa** - **boat** - /ō/ and **oe** - **toe** - /ō/. Present **ue** as **ue** - **blue** - /ü/, **ue** - **cue** - /ū/.

Notebook Entry
(Sound Section) The student must add **oa**, **oe** and **ue**

PART 2 Form the words | b | oa | t | and | t | oe | using the Sound Cards. Have the student tap and read these words (**boat** = 3 taps, **toe** = 2 taps). Tell him that these words have double vowels as well. Make the word **blue** and **cue** with Sound Cards. Remind him that the **u** has two long sounds, /ü/ and /ū/. Make some two-syllable words with Syllable Cards. Have the student decode the words (tap as needed).

PART 3   PART 4   PART 5   Follow the procedures for Parts 3, 4, and 5.

PART 6 Spread out all peach vowel cards taught thus far and a blank consonant card. Ask, "What says /ō/?" The student should pull down the cards **o**, **o** - blank - **e**, **oa**, and **oe**. "What says /ū/?" **u**, **u** - blank - **e**, and **ue**. "What says /ü/?" **u**, **u** - blank - **e**, and **ue**. Be sure he says the letter names as he finds the cards.

PART 7 Keep the spelling options for the sound /ō/ displayed. Make the following words: **coat**, **solo**, and **doe**. Explain that **oa** is the most common choice whenever the sound /ō/ is followed by a consonant. Ask the student to identify the words that end in the /ō/ sound. Isolate the words **solo** and **doe**. The most common way to spell /ō/ at the end of multisyllabic words is with **o**, the way they learned it first (**solo**). Next tell him that **oe** and **o** can end one-syllable words, and **o** ends open syllables within words (make **hoe**, **ho** and **hotel** and remark as you explain this). Dictate words with /ō/, including **o**, **o** - blank - **e**, **oa**, and **oe**. Later teach that the sounds /ü/ and /ū/ at the end of words are often spelled with **ue**. Make examples such as **true** and **rescue**. Dictate words with /ü/ and /ū/, using **u**, **u** - blank - **e**, and **ue** words. Have the student use a spell checker or dictionary to confirm his choices.

Notebook Entry
(Sound Section) The student should add to the chart for spelling options the sounds /ō/, /ü/, and /ū/.

PART 8   PART 9   PART 10   Follow the procedures for Parts 8, 9, and 10.

Weave with Questions
"Can you find the double vowel in this word?"

9.4   What to Teach

- The sounds of **oi**, **oy**, **au**, and **aw**

- How to read and spell words with the above sounds

Additional Materials Needed

- Sound Cards **oi**, **oy**, **au**, and **aw**

- 9.4 Syllable Cards, 9.4 Word Cards

 PART 1 Explain that there are more double vowels to learn. Show the student **oi** and **oy** cards. Tell him that these cards have the same sound. Say the letter names-keyword-sound for each and have the student repeat, "**oi** - **coin** - /oi/" and "**oy** - **boy** - /oi/." Then present the **au** and **aw** Sound Cards. Tell the student that these both say /ȯ/. Say letter names-keyword-sound for each and have the student repeat, "**au** - **autumn** - /ȯ/, **aw** - **saw** - /ȯ/."

Notebook Entry

(Sound Section) The student needs to add the sounds of **oi**, **oy**, **au**, and **aw** to his notebook.

 PART 2   **PART 3**   **PART 4**   **PART 5**   Follow the procedures for Parts 3, 4, and 5.

 PART 6 Be sure to ask, "What says /oi/?" and "What says /ȯ/?"

 PART 7 Teach the student to select **oy** and **aw** at the end of a word. Use the Sound Cards to demonstrate examples. Dictate one-syllable words with the new sounds. The student should use the Sound Cards (or blank cards) to spell the word. Be sure he orally spells the word after finding the cards.

Also dictate multisyllabic words. Use Syllable Cards for multisyllabic words. The dictionary or spell checker should be used as needed.

 PART 8   **PART 9**   **PART 10**   Follow the procedures for Parts 8, 9, and 10.

 ### Weave with Questions

Mark the syllable type: **boil**
                d

"What sound does the double vowel make?"

"What letters do you use at the end of a word to spell /oi/...(**oy**).../ȯ/...(**aw**)?"

9.5 What to Teach

- The sounds of **ow**, **ou** and **oo**

- How to read and spell words with the above sounds

Additional Materials Needed

- Sound Cards **ou**, **ow**, and **oo**

- 9.5 Syllable Cards, 9.5 Word Cards

PART 1 Tell the student that the next three double vowels are tricky because they each have two different sounds. Place the cards on the table or magnetic board:

Say the letter names-keywords-sounds for each card and have the student repeat:

ow - snow - /ō/, **ow** - plow - /ou/   **ou** - trout - /ou/, **ou** - soup - /ü/

oo - school - /ü/, **oo** - book - /u̇/

Point out that **ou** and **ow** share a sound (/ou/) and **ou** and **oo** share a sound (ü). If these cards are presented in this order it helps, since the last sound of **ow** is the first sound of **out** (**ou**). Then the last sound of **ou** is the first sound of **oo**.

Notebook Entry

(Sound Section) The student must add the three new double vowels to the vowel combination page.

PART 2 First make words with **ow**. Explain that whenever there is an **ow** in a word, it will either say /ō/ or /ou/. The student must determine the correct sound by trying both, as needed. If he is still unsure, he should check a dictionary or spell checker. After making and reading words with **ow**, do the same with **ou** and **oo**. Also, use Syllable Cards to make multisyllabic words.

PART 3   **PART 4**   **PART 5**   Follow the procedures for Parts 3, 4, and 5.

PART 6 Ask, "What says /ō/?" The student should find the following cards:

Ask, "What says /**ou**/?"

Ask, "What says /ü/?"

| u | u⬚e | ue | ou | oo |

Ask, "What says /u̇/"?

| oo |

Notebook Entry

(Sound Section) The student should add the new options to the spelling option pages.

PART 7 Dictate words with the aforementioned sounds. Do one sound at a time and spread out the cards for the options of that sound. For example, dictate /ō/ words. Spread out the cards as indicated above and have the student determine the correct option. Be sure to dictate words that are spelled with various options (such as **float**, **toe**, **snow**, **locate**, etc.).

Next dictate /**ou**/ words with the ⬚ow and ⬚ou cards displayed. Blank Syllable Cards can be used for multi-syllabic words. For example, if you dictate the word **discount**, the student should repeat the word and put out two blank Syllable Cards: ⬚⬚

He should place the blank vowel card on the syllable with the spelling option:

⬚⬚

Next, he should determine the correct option and spell the word, naming and spelling one syllable at a time. It is often necessary to write down both spellings, see which one looks right and then use the spell checker or dictionary to determine the correct one.

PART 8 PART 9 PART 10 Follow the procedures for Parts 8, 9, and 10.

Weave with Questions

"Circle the double vowel in the word."

"What sounds are made by that double vowel?"

"What are the two ways you might say that word? Which pronunciation is correct?"

Mark the "D" syllable type: t(ow)n
                              d

9.6   What to Teach

- The sounds of **ea**

- How to read and spell words with **ea**

Additional Materials Needed
- Sound Card **ea**

- 9.6 Syllable Cards, 9.6 Word Cards

 PART 1   Put the **ea** Sound Card on the table or magnetic board. Tell the student that this double vowel has three sounds. Say the letter names-keywords-sounds and have the student repeat:

ea - **eat** - /ē/   **ea** - **bread** - /ĕ/   **ea** - **steak** - /ā/

Notebook Entry

(Sound Section) The student must add the three sounds of **ea** into his sound section with the other double vowels.

 PART 2   Make words with the **ea** Sound Card and with Syllable Cards. Tell the student that the /ē/ sound of **ea** is the most common and should be tried first. The /ĕ/ sound should be tried if /ē/ does not make a word. Lastly, /ā/ is not very common and should be tried last. The student should check a dictionary or spell checker if unsure of the sound in a word.

 PART 3   **PART 4**   **PART 5**   Follow the procedures for Parts 3, 4, and 5.

 PART 6   The student should find the following cards.

Ask, "What says /ē/?"   e | y | ee | ey | ea

Ask, "What says /ĕ/?" e | ea

Ask, "What says /ā/?" a | ai | ay | ea

Notebook Section

(Sound Section) The student should add the new options to the spelling option pages.

 PART 7   Dictate words with above sounds, doing one sound at a time (see Part 7 in 9.5).

 PART 8   **PART 9**   **PART 10**   Follow the procedures for Parts 8, 9, and 10.

 Weave with Questions

"What are the three sounds of **ea**?"

"What does **ea** say in this word?"

Circle the double vowel.

Write the sound of **ea** above the double vowel.

$$\overset{/ē/}{\text{cr}\textcircled{ea}\text{m}}_{\text{d}}$$

9.7 What to Teach

- The sound of **ew**
- Advanced students: the sounds of **eu** and **ui**
- How to read and spell words with the above sounds

Additional Materials Needed
- Sound Cards **ew**, **eu**, **ui**
- 9.7 Syllable Cards, 9.7 Word Cards

PART 1

Present the new **ew** sound and tell the student that **ew** makes the two long sounds of **u** (/ū/ and /ü/). Say the keywords and have the student repeat, "**ew** - **few** - /ū/ and **ew** - **grew** - /ü/." For advanced students, teach that **eu** also says two long sounds of **u** (/ū/ and /ü/) and teach that **ui** says /ü/. Teach the keywords for **eu** and **ui**.

Notebook Entry

(Sound Section) The student needs to add the new sound(s) to the double vowel page of his notebook.

PART 2

Use the Sound Cards to make one-syllable words with the new sounds. These can be tapped out as needed. The word **few** would get two taps: /**f**/ - one tap, /ū/ - one tap. Also use Syllable Cards to make multisyllabic words with the new sounds. The student can use his finger to circle the vowel combinations while naming the sound. Then the multisyllabic word can be scooped and read.

PART 3

PART 4

PART 5

Follow the procedures for Parts 3, 4, and 5.

PART 6

Ask, "What says /ū/?" The student should select the cards:

    (advanced students)

Ask, "What says /ü/?" The student should select the above cards, with advanced students adding **ui**.

Notebook Entry

(Sound Section) The student should add the new spelling options for the sounds /ū/ and /ü/ to the sound option chart.

PART 7

Dictate words with the sounds /ū/ and /ü/. Include words with each spelling of the sound. Have the student determine the correct spelling option using a dictionary or spell checker, as needed.

Follow the procedures for Parts 8, 9, and 10.

Helpful Hints / Activities

The student can make a /ū/ or /ü/ chart (see Rules Notebook) on a large index card. He can determine the correct spellings by completing the chart as indicated below.

ex. "Spell **cute**."

u-e	u	ew	eu	ue
mule	**pupil**	**few**	**Europe**	**cue**
~~cute~~ (cute)	~~cut~~	~~cewt~~	~~ceut~~	~~cuet~~

Weave with Questions

"What letters say /ū/ (or /ü/) in this word?"

Step 10

At the end of this step, students should know:

- Exceptions to the v-e syllable: **ice**, **ace**, **age**, **ate**, **ile**, **ite**, **ine**

- How to add suffixes to words ending in a silent **e**

- How to identify 1:1:1 words [words with one syllable (closed or r-controlled) with one vowel followed by one consonant]

- How to add suffixes to multisyllabic words ending in an accented 1:1:1 syllable

- Additional suffixes: **-ic**, **-al**, **-ible**, **-ous**, **-ist**, **-ism**, **-ity**, **-ize**, **-ary**, **-ery**, **-ory**, **-ent**, **-ence**, **-ant**, **-ance**

The focus in Step 10 changes from work with sound options to spelling rules. The student will first learn additional exceptions to the v-e syllable. This prepares him for the silent **e** spelling rule. It is essential that this rule is practiced and mastered with Sound Cards and Suffix Cards. Next, the doubling spelling rules (or 1:1:1 rules) are taught. These, too, must be mastered with the Sound Cards and Suffix Cards. Lastly, advanced students learn additional vowel suffixes.

10.1 What to Teach

- Additional v-e exceptions: **ice**, **ace**, **age**, **ate**, **ite**, **ine**, **ile**

- How to read and spell words with above endings

Additional Materials Needed
- 10.1 Word Cards, 10.1 Syllable Cards

- Step 10 Student Reader and Student Rules Notebook

- Student Workbook 10A (optional)

PART 1

No new sounds are taught. Be sure to include the **g** and **c** consonant cards in the quick drill. Review the sounds of these letters when followed by **e**, **i**, **y**. Also be sure to include green **ive** card.

PART 2

Make the following words with Sound Cards:

Ask the student to explain why the **e** is at the end of each word (**give**: words in English do not end in **v** and **dance**: the **e** changes the sound of **c** to /**s**/.) Next ask which of the two words is a v-e syllable exception (**give**). In the word **give**, there is a vowel, then a consonant, then an **e**. Explain that the **e** should jump over the one consonant to make the **i** vowel long, but it doesn't. In 10.1 the student will learn additional vowel-consonant-e exceptions. Make the word **notice** with Sound Cards. Tell the student that there is a vowel-consonant-e in the word (point to cards), but the **e** is there only for the **c**. The sound of the **i** is short. Have him decode the word. Make the word **palace** and then **damage**. Explain that the **e** in each of these words is there for the **c** or the **g**. The preceding vowels actually sound like a short **i** (/ĭ/). Make additional words with Syllable Cards for the student to decode. When the above vowel-consonant-e exceptions have been mastered, use the Sound Cards to form the words **private**, **favorite**, and **engine**. Point out the vowel-consonant-e in each word. Explain that **ate**, **ite**, and **ine** are sometimes word endings. Read the words and then have students read them. Make additional words with Syllable Cards for the student to practice. (There are a few words with **ile** as well, such as **fertile**. Most of these words are B Level vocabulary).

Notebook Entry
(Syllable Section) Add the additional v-e exceptions to the vowel-consonant-e syllable type in the syllable section of the notebook.

PART 3

Follow the procedure for Part 3.

PART 4

Be sure to identify the specific v-e exception at the end of the words. Practice in Parts 2 and 3 before presenting the wordlist in the reader.

Follow the procedures for Parts 5 and 6.

PART 7   Put out blank Syllable Cards.

 Use Syllable Cards to make 10.1 words. Turn the Syllable Cards face down and dictate the word. For example, put the Syllable Cards for the word **service** face down:

Dictate the word. The student should repeat the word in syllables and spell one syllable at a time. A dictionary or spell checker should be used to check spellings for the **ice** versus **ace**, and **ite** versus **ate** (tell the student that the **ate** is much more frequent). Make additional words with Syllable Cards to practice spelling. There are several words with doubled consonants, such as **office**, **cabbage**, **cottage**. Remind the student that the extra consonant helps to close in the first vowel to give it a short sound.

PART 8 PART 9  PART 10   Follow the procedures for Parts 8, 9, and 10.

 Helpful Hints / Activities

It might be helpful to make green cards for each word ending. Use green cards for each word ending. The student can say the letters-keyword-sound:

ice - **notice** - /ĭs/   **age** - **damage** - /ĭj/   **ite** - **favorite** - /ĭt/

ace - **palace** - /ĭs/   **ate** - **pirate** - /ĭt/   **ine** - **engine** - /ĭn/

ile - **fertile** - /ĭl/

Notes / FYI

There are a group of **ate** words that have two pronunciations. One pronunciation follows the v-e rule and the other does not. When used as a verb, the word has a long vowel sound (**duplicate**, **estimate**, **advocate**). When used as a noun, the word has the vowel-consonant-e exception (**duplicate**, **estimate**, **advocate**). This group of words can be presented to advanced students and can be found on a B wordlist in the Student Reader.

The **age** exception is sometimes a suffix that can be added to a word that stands alone (such as **pass** - **passage**, **post** - **postage**). The other exceptions are word endings added to roots.

Weave with Questions

Have students mark v-e exceptions:

ser vĭce   sĕn ăte
   v×e   v×e

10.2 What to Teach

- How to add suffixes to words ending in silent **e**

- How to read and spell silent **e** words with suffixes

Additional Materials Needed
- 10.2 Word Cards

- Suffix Cards previously learned

No new sounds are added. Have the student read previously taught Suffix Cards.

First have the student categorize suffixes into two columns, putting the suffixes that begin with a vowel in one column and the suffixes that begin with a consonant in another column. Make the word **hope** with the Sound Cards:

Tell the student that words ending in silent **e** follow a rule when adding a vowel suffix. Put the **ing** Suffix Card beside the word **hope**. Tell the student that whenever a vowel suffix (point to vowel suffixes) is added to a word with a silent **e**, the **e** must drop from the end. Pull down the silent **e** card and move the **ing** Suffix Card over to form **hoping**. Put the **ing** back and make **hope** again. Tell the student that whenever a consonant suffix is added to a silent **e** word, the suffix is simply added and the **e** does not drop. Add the suffixes -**ful** and -**less** to demonstrate. Next explain that this rule applies no matter why there is a silent **e** at the end of a word. Make various words and discuss the silent **e**, add suffixes to these words, and explain the addition of the vowel versus consonant suffixes. Some word examples include:

Word	Silent e	Addition of suffixes
give	exception: no word ends in **v**	**giving**, **giver**
settle	consonant-le syllable	**settling**, **settler**, **settlement**
manage	exception: **e** there for the **g**	**managing**, **manager**, **management**
nice	**e**: two jobs: v-e and **c** /**s**/	**nicest**, **nicer**, **nicely**

Be sure to demonstrate the above words with Sound Cards and Suffix Cards. This helps the student understand the dropping of the **e** since the **e** is literally dropped whenever the vowel suffix is added.

Advanced Students
Explain that words with **ge** and **ce** sometimes need to keep the **e** even when adding a vowel suffix. Make the word **trace** with the Sound Cards. Ask the student the sound of **c** /**s**/. Add the suffix -**ing**, dropping the **e** to make **tracing**. Ask the student the sound of **c** (/**s**/). Ask if the **i** in the suffix -**ing** can make **c** say /**s**/ (yes). Now put the -**ing** suffix back and put the **e** back to make **trace**. Add the vowel suffix able to form **traceable**. Ask the student whether or not the **e** drops when adding a vowel suffix.

Drop the **e** to form **tracable**. Ask if the **c** says /**s**/ when followed by the letter **a** (point to the letter). Remind the student that **c** says /**s**/ only when followed by **e, i** and **y**. Put the **e** back to make **traceable**. Explain that the **e** doesn't drop in this word so that the **c** will say /**s**/. Form similar words with **g** such as **changeable** and discuss them.

PART 3 Have the student read these words naming the baseword first, then the whole word. For example, the word **hoping** should be read "**hope, hoping**." Initially model this for the student since this is somewhat difficult for the words with the vowel suffixes added.

PART 4 The student must read the baseword first, then the whole word "**brave, bravest**."

PART 5 **PART 6** Follow the procedures for Parts 5 and 6.

PART 7 The student should categorize suffixes into two columns (see Part 2). Dictate 10.2 words. Be sure to dictate the entire word, then have the student name the baseword. For example, if you dictate the word **hoping**, the student repeats "**hoping**" then names the baseword, "**hope**."

PART 8 **PART 9** **PART 10** Follow the procedures for Parts 8, 9, and 10.

Notebook Entry
(Spelling Section) The student must add the silent **e** spelling rule to his notebook.

Weave with Questions
"What is the baseword?"

"Do you drop the **e**?" "Why or why not?"

When doing words such as **changeable** with advanced students, ask, "Why doesn't the **e** drop when this vowel suffix is added?"

10.3   What to Teach

- How to identify closed and r-controlled words with one syllable and one consonant following the single vowel (called 1:1:1 words)

- How to add suffixes to the words described above

Additional Materials Needed
- 10.3 Word Cards

- Blank white index cards to make extra consonants

PART 1   Follow the procedure for Part 1.

PART 2   First, present the student with a mixed, fat stack of Word Cards from previous steps. The student must go through the stack and find all the one-syllable words. Put aside any multisyllabic words. Next, spread out all the one-syllable words. The student should select all the closed syllable and r-controlled syllable words. Put the other words aside. Now select one of the words from the remaining Word Cards (the closed syllable and the r-controlled syllable words). Make the selected word with Sound Cards. For example, if the word on the Word Card is **thump**, use the Sound Cards to form the word: th u m p

Now ask the following questions:

"Is this a one-syllable word?" (Yes)

"Is it either closed or r-controlled?" (Yes)

"Is there only one consonant after the vowel?" (No)

Select a Word Card that has only one consonant after the vowel. Make that word with the Sound Cards (for example, the word **thin**). Ask the same three questions. The answer will be "Yes" for all three questions. Tell the student that the word is a special kind of word called a 1:1:1 word. It has only one syllable that is either a closed or r-controlled syllable, it has only one vowel, and the vowel is followed by only one consonant. Have the student find any other Word Cards that are 1:1:1 words. Put the other words aside.

Next have the student categorize the vowel and consonant suffixes into two columns. Select a 1:1:1 word on a Word Card such as **thin**. Tell the student that when a suffix is added to the 1:1:1 words, sometimes the baseword changes to add the suffix. Ask the student which kind of suffix can simply be added without worrying about changing the word (consonant suffix). Add **ly** to form **thinly**. Tell the students that consonant suffixes are simply added to these words. Next tell the student that whenever a vowel suffix is added to 1:1:1. words, the last consonant is doubled. Add the -**er** suffix to **thin: thin** -**er**. Make another **n** on an index card and add it to form **thinner**.

Repeat this with the word **hop ing**. Explain that this word would be **hoping** if the extra **p** wasn't added. The extra consonant helps to keep the vowel short in closed syllables. Explain that the consonant doubles in the r-controlled words, too, but the vowel keeps the r-controlled sound. Demonstrate with **star**, **starry**, **starring**, **starred**. Without the double **r**, the word **starring** would be **staring**.

Note: For many students it is helpful to do the above work in several lessons. First be sure the student becomes proficient at finding 1:1:1 words. Provide practice with the workbook pages and make wordlists for students to find and circle 1:1:1 words. When the student can easily identify these words, proceed to the suffix additions.

PART 3 The words on Word Cards should be read with the baseword, then the whole word (**hopping** should be read, "**hop** - **hopping**").

PART 4 The words on the wordlists should be read with the baseword, then the whole word ("**hop** - **hopping**".)

PART 5 **PART 6** Follow the procedures for Parts 5 and 6.

PART 7 The student should categorize the suffixes into two columns. Dictate a one-syllable word. Have the student form the word with Sound Cards. Ask whether or not the word is a 1:1;1 word. Next dictate the word with a suffix. Have the student add the suffix to form the word. If needed, the student should use a blank white index card to make an additional consonant. Remind the student that only 1:1:1 words have the final consonant double when adding a vowel suffix. The **w** in the word **show** does not double when **ing** is added since it is not a 1:1:1 word.

Notebook Entry
(Spelling Section) The student must add the 1:1:1 Doubling Rule Part 1 to his notebook.

PART 8 **PART 9** **PART 10** Follow the procedures for Parts 8, 9, and 10.

Notes / FYI
There are certain consonants that do not double in English words (**j**, **k**, **v**, **w**, **x**, and **y**). Have the student add this to his notebook, but tell him that the **x** is the only consonant that will end a 1:1:1 word (such as **fix**). Practice spelling words with **x** such as **fixing**, **mixer**, etc.

Weave with Questions
"Find any 1:1:1 word."

"Why is the consonant doubled in this word?"

"Why isn't the consonant doubled in this word?"

The student can mark these words: tell him to underline the baseword, circle the suffix and cross out the extra consonant since it is silent.

10.4 What to Teach

- Doubling Rule Part II (to advanced students only)
- How to recognize multisyllabic words with final 1:1:1 accented syllables
- How to add suffixes to the above words

Additional Materials Needed
- 10.4 Word Cards
- Make Syllable Cards for the following words: **forget**, **silver**, **consult**, **admit**, **conceal**
- Blank white index cards

 PART 1 Follow the procedure for Part 1.

  PART 2 Display the following words in syllables:

| for | get | | sil | ver | | con | sult | | ad | mit | | con | ceal |

Ask the student to point to and read the final syllable in each word. Next ask him to point to any of the final syllables that follow the 1:1:1 pattern (**get, ver, mit**). Ask why **sult** and **ceal** do not follow the 1:1:1 pattern (**sult** has two consonants after the single vowel and **ceal** has two vowels and is not closed or r-controlled). Remove **consult** and **conceal**. Tell the student that multisyllabic words that end in a 1:1:1 syllable sometimes double the final consonant when a vowel suffix is added. Have the student categorize suffixes into two columns. Ask the student to point to the column of suffixes that are simply added to words (the consonant suffixes). Add **ful** to **forget** to form **forgetful**.

Next tell the student that there is an additional question to ask before doubling the final consonant in multisyllabic words. This additional consideration makes it very tricky. Explain that the final syllable must be a 1:1:1 syllable and it must be the accented syllable as well. Read each word with the student, stressing or accenting first one syllable, then the other syllable, to hear which one is correct.

In other words, first read the word **forget** as **for´ get** then **for get´** to hear that the correct pronunciation is **forget´**. Determine the accent for each word and mark the Syllable Card with an accent mark:

| for | get´ | | sil´ | ver | | ad | mit´ |

Next add suffixes to each word to demonstrate the doubling rule. Make an additional consonant with an index card as needed and discuss each word that you make. Examples include:

forgetting: double the **t** because get is an accented 1:1:1 syllable and a vowel suffix is added

silvery: **r** is not doubled because even though **ver** is a 1:1:1 syllable, it is not accented

admitted: double the **t** because **mit** is an accented 1:1:1 syllable and a vowel suffix is added

PART 3

The Word Cards should be read with the baseword first, then the whole word "**forget** - **forgetting**."

PART 4

The words on the wordlist should be read with the baseword first, then the whole word "**forget** - **forgetting**."

PART 5   PART 6

Follow the procedures for Parts 5 and 6.

PART 7

Dictate a 10.4 word including the suffix. Have the student repeat the whole word and then name the baseword. For example, say the word **admitting**. The student then says, "**admitting** - **admit**." Have him pull down blank Syllable Cards for the baseword and the correct Suffix Card:

Next have him write the baseword on the Syllable Cards and determine the accent:

ad	mit´

Ask him if the second syllable is 1:1:1 (yes) and then ask him if it is accented (yes). If the answer is yes to each question have him make an additional consonant as needed:

Notebook Entry

(Spelling Section) The student should add the Doubling Rule Part II

PART 8   PART 9   PART 10

Follow the procedures for Parts 8, 9, and 10.

Notes / FYI

Words ending in **ic**: rather then double the **c**, add a **k** to form **ck** before adding a vowel suffix beginning with **e** or **i**. The **e** or **i** would change the sound of **c** to /**s**/. Thus **picnic** + **ing** = **picni<u>ck</u>ing** not **picni<u>cc</u>ing**.

The Doubling Rule Part II is quite difficult due to the accent. Some students are unable to hear the stressed syllable. In that case, the student should check the dictionary for any multisyllabic word that ends in a 1:1:1 syllable. The important thing will be to determine words that have final syllables that are potential ones for doubling and only check those words. For example, a word such as **conceal** would not need to be checked, but a word such as **begin** should be checked.

Weave with Questions

"Why does the consonant double in this word?"

"Why doesn't the consonant double in this word?"

"Which syllable is accented?"

10.5 What to Teach

- Additional suffixes: **-ic, -al, -ible, -ous, -ist, -ism, -ity, -ize, -ary, -ery, -ory, -ent, -ence, -ant, -ance** (advanced students)

Additional Materials Needed
- 10.5 Syllable Cards (suffixes), 10.5 Word Cards

PART 1 Follow the procedure for Part 1.

PART 2 Ask the student to brainstorm as many vowel suffixes and consonant suffixes as possible. Display suffixes as the student names them. Tell him that there are many suffixes in the English language. Display the 10.5 Suffix Cards. Note that these are all vowel suffixes. Next read each suffix and have the student repeat it. Say a word with the suffix and have the student repeat the word then name the baseword. Next tell the student that the silent **e** and the 1:1:1 spelling rules apply when adding these suffixes to basewords. Make the word **cube** with Sound Cards. Add the suffix **ic** (drop the **e**) to make the word **cubic**.

Explain that two suffixes can be added to a baseword. Remind the student that he has already done this with words such as **helpfully**. Make the word **helpfully**. Point out the two suffixes. Make the word **real** with Sound Cards. Add the **-ist** suffix and have the student read the word. Next add **ic** to make **realistic**. Have the student read the baseword then the whole word. Add **al** and **ly** to form **realistically**. This word starts with the baseword **real**. Suffixes are added to change the part of speech or to change how a word is used in a sentence. Use the words **real, realist, realistic,** and **realistically** in sentences to demonstrate.

Notebook Entry
(Spelling Section) The additional suffixes must be added in the student's spelling section.

PART 3 Be sure student reads the baseword, then the whole word.

PART 4 Be sure student reads the baseword, then the whole word.

PART 5 **PART 6** Follow the procedures for Parts 5 and 6.

PART 7 Use blank Syllable Cards and Suffix Cards. Dictate a 10.5 word. The student should repeat the whole word then name the baseword. Next the student should pull down blank Syllable Cards to represent the baseword and attach the needed suffix(es). Lastly, the word should be spelled by syllable. Remind the student to apply spelling rules as needed.

PART 8 PART 9 PART 10 Follow the procedures for Parts 8, 9, and 10.

Notes / FYI

Some words change pronunciation with the addition of the suffix. Sometimes this is due to an accent shift (**prefer** - **preference, organ** - **organic**). You can model the correct pronunciation to help the student whenever this occurs. Some words change due to the **c** followed by a suffix that begins with an **i** (**critic** - **criticism, romantic** - **romanticism, authentic** - **authenticity**). Make these with cards to demonstrate.

Some students are able to learn generalizations that help determine the correct suffix. Teach these generalizations as appropriate. Otherwise, the student can use option spelling procedures to determine the correct suffix.

Further Information Regarding Suffix Choice

est vs. **ist**
- **est** is used as a comparative adjective (**quickest**)
- **ist** is used for a person (**motorist**)

ible vs. **able**
- **ible** is used with Latin roots when the word doesn't stand alone (**audible**) and with words that have corresponding words ending in **tion, sion,** or **ive** (**collection** - **collectible, destructive** - **destructible**)
- **ation** words correspond to **able**

ant / ance vs. **ent / ence**
- **ent / ence** used to keep **c** and **g** soft (**urgent, indulgence**) used after Latin roots:

her	-	adherence, coherent
cur	-	occurrence
spond	-	respondent, despondence
sist	-	consistent, persistent (exceptions to this = assistance, resistant)
fer	-	conference, inference (an exception to this = sufferance)

(There are additional generalizations but these are most helpful.)

Weave with Questions
"What is the baseword?"
"What is the suffix?"
Have students circle suffixes: **convert(ible)**
If a silent **e** has been dropped from baseword, indicate it by using a caret: **festiv(al)**

Step 11

At the end of this step, students should know:

- All sounds of **y** as a vowel (**y** = /ī/, /ĭ/, /ē/)
- How to read **y** in various syllable types
- The '**y**' spelling rule (when to change **y** to **i** when adding suffixes)
- Variant sounds of **i** (**i** = /ē/ and /**y**/)
- The sounds of **ie**, **ei**, **igh** and **eigh**, and how to read and spell words with these sounds

Step Eleven focuses on additional vowel work. The vowels **y** and **i** are studied in further detail. The student will also learn how to add suffixes and how to pluralize words ending in **y**. Lastly, additional 'doubled vowels' will be studied. Two of these have more than two letters (**igh** and **eigh**). These vowel combinations, however, can still be grouped with the "D" syllable.

11.1 What to Teach

- The vowel **y** in a closed syllable says /ĭ/
- The vowel **y** in an open syllable at the end of multisyllabic words usually says /ē/ but sometimes says /ī/ (advanced students)
- The vowel **y** in a v-e syllable says /ī/ (advanced students)

Additional Materials Needed
- 11.1 Syllable Cards, 11.1 Word Cards
- Step 11 Student Reader and Student Rules Notebook
- Student Workbook 11A (optional)

 PART 1

In the first lesson, do not include the new sounds of **y** until after Part 2. Then present the **y** vowel card and have student repeat:

y - **y** - **cry** - /ī/

y - **y** - **baby** - /ē/

y - **y** - **reply** - /ī/ (advanced students)

y - **y** - **gym** - /ĭ/

y - **y** - **type** - /ī/ (advanced students)

Notebook Entry

(Sound Section) The new sounds of **y** must be added to the appropriate vowel pages of the student's notebook.

 PART 2

Present the **y** vowel card. Have the student name the sounds of the **y** vowel taught thus far (**y** - **cry** - /ī/, **y** - **baby** - /ē/). Ask the student to name the type of syllable that the **y** is in for the words **cry** and **baby** (open).

Advanced Students

Teach that **y** in an open syllable at the end of the word usually says /ē/ as they previously learned. However, **y** sometimes says /ī/ at the end of multisyllabic words. Make the word **reply**. Tell the student that the **y** in this word says /ī/. Make additional words to demonstrate.

All Students

Explain that the vowel **y** can also be found in closed syllables. Make the word **gym** with the Sound Cards. Ask if the vowel is long or short in a closed syllable (short). Tell the student that **y** has the short sound /ĭ/ in a closed syllable. Make additional words to practice.

Advanced Students

Teach that **y** can also be found in v-e syllables. Make the word **type** with Sound Cards. Ask if the vowel is long or short in a v-e syllable (long). Tell the student that **y** says /ī/ in a v-e syllable. Make additional words to practice.

 PART 3   **PART 4**   **PART 5**

Follow the procedures for Parts 3, 4, and 5.

PART 6 Ask, "What says /ĭ/?" In response, the student should find the **i** and **y** cards. Ask the student to name the kind of syllable that makes these vowels have the short sound (closed). Ask, "What says /ī/?" In response, the student should find:

   (advanced students)

PART 7 Dictate words with /ĭ/ and /ī/ vowel sounds. The students should use the dictionary or spell checker to determine the correct spelling option for these sounds. Explain that the vowel **y** is far less common.

Notebook Entry

(Sound Section) The student should add the spelling options for /ĭ/ and /ī/.

PART 8   PART 9   PART 10   Follow the procedures for Parts 8, 9, and 10.

Weave with Questions

"What kind of syllable is the **y** in?"

"What is the sound of **y**?"

The student should mark these syllables:

g**y**m   t**y**pe
  c   e

11.2 What to Teach

- How to add suffixes to words ending in **y**

- How to form the plural for words ending in **y**

Additional Materials Needed

- Make an -**s** Suffix Card on a yellow index card

- 11.2 Syllable Cards, 11.2 Word Cards

- Word Cards ending in **y** from previous steps

- Blank index cards

PART 1

Follow the procedure for Part 1.

PART 2

Have the student categorize suffixes into two columns (vowel and consonant). Add the -**s** Suffix Card to the consonant column. Present the student with a fat stack of Word Cards ending in **y** (such as **donkey**, **baby**, **boy**, **cry**, etc.). Make additional cards as needed. Be sure to include several that end in a "double vowel" (**ey**, **ay**, **oy**), and several that end in an open syllable. Instruct the student to make two piles: a pile with **y** in a "D" syllable and a pile with **y** in an open syllable. Select a word from the "D" syllable pile (such as **boy**). Tell the student that whenever a suffix is added to a word ending in **y** in a "D" syllable, the suffix is simply added. It does not matter whether it is a vowel or a consonant suffix. Demonstrate with an example such as **boys** and **boyish**. Add suffixes to several words from the "D" pile. Next select a word from the pile that has **y** at the end of a word in an open syllable (such as **baby**). Explain that whenever a suffix is added to a word that ends in **y** in an open syllable, the **y** changes to **i** before the suffix is added. Demonstrate by covering the **y** with the **i** Sound Card and adding a suffix. Tell the student that this happens with both vowel and consonant suffixes.

baby - **babied**

Show them that the **y** does not change to **i** if the suffix begins with **i** since this would be awkward.

baby - **babyish**, not **babiish**

Tell the student that to make words plural (more than one), add **s** if **y** is in a "D" syllable, and change the **y** to **i** and add **es** if **y** is in an open syllable. Demonstrate several words from each pile.

baby - **babies**

PART 3

The student should read the baseword then the whole word. **Valleys** is read "**valley** - **valleys**" and **luckiest** is read, "**lucky** - **luckiest**."

PART 4

The student should read the baseword then the whole word. **Valleys** is read "**valley** - **valleys**" and **luckiest** is read, "**lucky** - **luckiest**."

Follow the procedures for Parts 5 and 6.

 Categorize Suffix Cards. Use blank index cards for the syllables in the basewords that you dictate. Dictate a 11.2 word such as **delayed**. Have the student repeat the word then name the baseword ("**de-layed - delay**"). Next he should represent the syllables in the baseword with blank index cards and add the needed suffix: -**ed**.

Have the students orally spell the baseword one syllable at a time. He should use the dictionary or spell checker as needed. Have him write the word on the Syllable Cards. If the word ends in a "D" syllable, have him just add the suffix. If it ends in an open syllable, have him cover the **y** with the **i** Sound Card and add the suffix. Be sure to dictate words that are plurals (some adding **s** and some changing **y** to **i** and adding **es**).

Notebook Entry

(Spelling Section) The student must add the "**y**" spelling rule and the plural rules to his notebook.

Note: There are additional plural rules listed in the Rules Notebook. These can be added and discussed with the student as appropriate.

   Follow the procedures for Parts 8, 9, and 10.

 Notes / FYI

When the **y** changes to **i**, it retains the sound it made in the original word. The **y** can say /ī/ or /ē/ in an open syllable.

baby - **y** says /ē/; change **y** to **i** - **babied** (**i** says /ē/)

try - **y** says /ī/; change **y** to **i** - **trīed** (**i** says /ī/)

Be sure to discuss this and apply it when reading the words with **i** replacing **y**.

 Weave with Questions

"What type of syllable ends that word?"

"Do you just add the suffix or change the **y** to **i**?" "Why?"

The student should mark these words:

tom b**oy**s   ba b**ies**   cit **ies**

11.3 What to Teach

- Two new sounds of **i**: **i** = /**y**/ and **i** =/**ē**/

Additional Materials Needed
- 11.3 Syllable Cards, 11.3 Word Cards

PART 1

In the first lesson, do not include the new sounds of **i** in the quick drill. After Part 2, hold up the **i** vowel card and say the following and have the student repeat:

[i] - **itch** - /ĭ/

[i] - **pine** - /ī/

[i] - **hi** - /ī/

[i] - **compliment** - /ə/

[i] - **million** - /y/

[i] - **champion** - /ē/

Notebook Entry
(Sound Section) The sound of **i** as in **champion** should be added to the open syllable vowel page. The sound of **i** as in **million** should be added to the spelling option page.

PART 2

Present the **i** Sound Card. Ask the student to name the sounds of **i** learned thus far. Next tell him that **i** is sometimes followed by another vowel. Even though there are two vowels in a row (double vowels), it is not a "D" syllable. The **i** says either /y/ or /ē/.

Use Sound Cards to make the words **million** and **champion**. Cover the **i** in **million** with the consonant **y** card (white, not peach). Cover the **i** in **champion** with the **e** vowel card. Read the words and point out the sound of **i** in each word. Next explain that **i** often says /ē/ if it is followed by another vowel. The syllables are split between the two vowels:

/ē/

cham pi on
  c   ✗   c

Explain that **i** might say /y/ if it comes after an **l** or an **n** (such as in **million** and **onion**). Make additional words to demonstrate. Have the student cover the **i** with either the consonant **y** card or the **e** vowel card and then read the word.

Advanced Students
Tell the students that several prefixes end with the letter **i** saying /ē/. Make prefix cards for the following prefixes: **mini-, anti-, semi-, omni-, multi-, ambi-**. Read these and have the student repeat. Add these prefixes to words and have the student read them. Discuss meaning as you present these prefixes.

PART 3   **PART 4**   **PART 5**   Follow the procedures for Parts 3, 4, and 5.

PART 6   Ask the student, "What says /**y**/?" (**y**, **i**) "When will **i** say /**y**/?" (after an **n** or **l** and followed by another vowel)

Also ask, "What says /**ē**/?" The answer must now include **i**: **e-e, e, y, ee, ey, ea, i**

Ask, "When will **i** say /**ē**/?" (when it is followed by another vowel. Advanced students should add, "At the end of some prefixes.")

PART 7   Dictate 11.3 words. The student can spell these words with the Sound Cards or with blank Syllable Cards. The dictionary or a spell checker should be used to check the spelling.

PART 8   **PART 9**   **PART 10**   Follow the procedures for Parts 8, 9, and 10.

Notes / FYI

Long /ī/ was historically pronounced like our present day /ē/. In the Great Vowel Shift of the 14th century, change occurred.

The letter **i** is a connective between roots and suffixes. The word, however, does not 'stand alone' when the suffix is removed.

Word	Root	Connective	Suffix
menial =	**me**	**ni**	**al**

Weave with Questions

"What does the **i** say in this word?"

Have the student write the sound of **i** above the letter **i**:

$\overset{\text{y}}{\underline{\text{mil}}}$ $\underline{\text{li}\breve{\text{on}}}$ $\underline{\text{cham}}$ $\overset{/ē/}{\underline{\text{pi}}}$ $\underline{\text{on}}$
  c   c   c   ⊗   c

11.4 What to Teach

- Sounds of **ie** and **ei**
- How to use spelling option procedures to spell **ie** and **ei** words

Additional Materials Needed
- Sound Cards **ie** and **ei**
- 11.4 Syllable Cards, 11.4 Word Cards

PART 1

In the first lesson, do not include the new Sound Cards **ie** and **ei** in the quick drill. After Part 2, present these cards and say the letters-keywords-sounds and have the student repeat:

ie - **ie** - **piece** /ē/

ei - **ei** - **ceiling** /ē/

ei - **ei** - **vein** /ā/

Include these Sound Cards in subsequent lessons.

Notebook Entry

(Sound Section) The student should add **ie** and **ei** to his list of double vowels.

PART 2

Review the "D" syllable type, making some words with the Sound Cards. Have the student read the words and identify the double vowel by circling it with his index finger. Present the **ie** and **ei** Sound Cards and explain that these are two additional vowel combinations. First teach **ie**. Say, "i-e - **piece** - /ē/," and have the students repeat. Explain that **ie** says /ē/. Make several words to practice. Tell him that in a few words **ie** says /ī/, but there are so few these are learned as sight words (**die**, **lie**, **pie**, and **tie**).

Next present **ei** and tell the student that this double vowel has two sounds: /ē/ and /ā/. Make **ei** words. The student should try the /ē/ sound first. If the word does not sound familiar then he should try the /ā/ sound. Use a dictionary or spell checker as needed to determine the correct sound.

PART 3   **PART 4**   **PART 5**

Follow the procedures for Parts 3, 4, and 5.

PART 6

Spread out vowel cards. Ask, "What says /ē/?" The student should pull down the following:

Also ask, "What says /ā/?" The student should pull down the following:

Notebook Entry

(Sound Section) The student should add the **ie** to the /ē/ spelling option chart, and the **ei** to the /ē/ and /ā/ spelling option charts.

PART 7 First spread out the Sound Cards for /ē/ (see Part 6). Dictate words with /ē/. Explain that both **ie** and **ei** are options for spelling /ē/ within a word. The **ei** should be used after the letter **c**. Also, **ie** is an option for spelling /ē/ at the end of the word, although it is less common than **y** or **ey**.

Next, spread out the Sound Cards for /ā/ (see Part 6).

Explain that the **ei** is an option for spelling /ā/ although it is quite rare. Dictate various words with the /ā/ sound (some with **ei** and some with other options). The student should use a dictionary or spell checker as needed.

PART 8   **PART 9**   **PART 10**   Follow the procedures for Parts 8, 9, and 10.

Notes / FYI

There is a well-known saying, "**i** before **e** except after **c** or when sounding like /ā/ as in **neighbor** or **weigh**." This has several exceptions; thus it might be best to simply tell the student **ie** is more common unless after **c**.

Helpful Hints / Activities

Have the student make a chart such as the one below. Dictate /ē/ words and have him determine the correct column to place it into.

e-e	e	y	ee	ea	ey	i	ie	e
		candy	bleed	steam			belief	

Weave with Questions

Syllables with **ie** and **ei** are "D" syllables and should be marked:

r̄e lief   vein
o   d   d

Circle the double vowel. "What does it say?"

11.5 What to Teach

- Sounds of **igh** and **eigh**

- How to use sound option spelling procedures to spell **igh** and **eigh** words

Additional Materials Needed
- Sound Cards **igh** and **eigh**

- 11.5 Syllable Cards, 11.5 Word Cards

 PART 1

In the first lesson, do not include the new Sound Cards **igh** and **eigh** in the quick drill. After Part 2, present these cards and say the letters-keywords-sounds and have the students repeat:

 - **light** - /ī/   **eigh** - **eight** - /ā/

Include these Sound Cards in subsequent lessons.

Notebook Entry
(Sound Section) The student should add **igh** and **eigh** to his list of double vowels.

 PART 2

Present the two new Sound Cards: **igh** and **eigh**. Tell the student that these two vowel combinations each have one sound. Even though there are more than two letters, they belong to the "D" syllable type. The letters all stay together to make a sound. The **igh** says /ī/ and the **eigh** says /ā/. Tell the student that **eigh** is the strangest combination of letters since it takes four letters to say /ā/ and not even one of the four letters is an **a**. Make words with both **igh** and **eigh**. Have the student circle the vowel combination, name its sound and then read the word.

 PART 3   **PART 4**   **PART 5**

Follow the procedures for Parts 3, 4, and 5.

 PART 6

Spread out vowel cards. Ask, "What says /ī/?" The student should pull down the following:

(for advanced students)

Also ask, "What says /ā/?" The student should pull down the following:

Notebook Entry
(Sound Section) The student should add the **igh** to the /ī/ spelling option chart and the **eigh** to the /ā/ spelling option chart.

PART 7 First spread out the Sound Cards for /ī/ (see Part 6). Explain that **igh** is an option for /ī/. It is usually followed by the letter **t**. Dictate /ī/ words and have the student determine spelling (include **igh** words as well as words spelled with other /ī/ options).

Next, put out the Sound Cards for /ā/ (see Part 6). Explain that **eigh** is an option for /ā/. It is only used in a very small number of words (**eight**, **weigh**, **sleigh**, **freight**, **neigh**, **neighbor** and derivatives). Dictate /ā/ words (including **eigh** words as well as words spelled with other /ā/ options).

The spell checker or dictionary should be used as needed to determine the correct spelling.

PART 8   **PART 9**   **PART 10**   Follow the procedures for Parts 8, 9, and 10.

Weave with Questions
Syllables with **igh** and **eigh** should be marked:

   s(igh)t   w(eigh)t
     d   d

Step 12

At the end of this step, students should know:

- The exception to the "D" syllable: how to divide syllables between two vowels
- Silent letters: **rh, gh, mb, mn, kn, gn, wr**
- How /**w**/ effects the vowels **a** and **o**
- Two additional ways to spell /**k**/: **ch, que**
- The sounds of **ti, ci, tu**, and **ture**
- How to add prefixes to Latin roots

Step 12 presents additional information about word structure. This includes exceptions to the "D" syllable, silent letters, the effect of **w** on vowels, advanced spelling of /**k**/ sound, work with **ti, ci, tu**, and **ture** and the introduction to chameleon prefixes. The study of Latin roots, prefixes and suffixes can be quite extensive. The student is introduced to this in Step 12. At the completion of Step 12, the student is prepared for a more in-depth study of word structure, if desired.

When a student completes the twelve steps it is a major accomplishment for both the teacher and student! If the teacher presented the steps slowly enough for automaticity, the student should be prepared to decode just about anything. Practice is required for fluency. It is essential to continue reading with the student in non-controlled texts. With practice, reading rate will increase and the student should become more and more proficient. An extremely dyslexic student may never read at a normal rate. He will, however, be able to determine the words on the page independently. These students often need taped texts in order to keep up with the amount of reading required in their classes.

Again, congratulations for the completion of this extensive work.

12.1 What to Teach

- Exceptions to the "D" syllable: split vowels
- How to read and spell words with split vowels

Additional Materials Needed
- 12.1 Syllable Cards, 12.1 Word Cards
- Blank index cards
- Step 12 Student Reader and Student Rules Notebook
- Student Workbook 12A (optional)

 PART 1   Follow the procedure for Part 1.

 PART 2   Review the six syllable types and exceptions for the first five types (see Rules Notebook). Explain that the "D" syllable also has exceptions. Make the word **poet** with the Sound Cards, dividing the word into syllables. Have the student read each syllable, then put them together to decode the word. Point to the two vowels in the word and tell the student that in some words, there are two vowels together that split rather than stay together. Remind the student that he already studied words such as **radio**. The words in 12.1 also contain two consecutive vowels that split into two different syllables. Most of these must be learned through experience. Some, however, contain two vowels together that are never digraphs or diphthongs. In other words, they never stay together to form a double vowel. Examples include **io** (**violet**, **lion**), **ia** (**trial**, **dial**) and **ua** (**evacuate**, **Joshua**). Make some words with Sound Cards and have the student split the words between the two vowels and then decode them. Also, present the words with Syllable Cards and have the student read each syllable to decode the words.

Advanced Students

Explain that some prefixes end in a vowel in an open syllable. Open syllable prefixes include:

pre   **co**   **re**

di   **tri**   **de**   **pro**

Write these prefixes on index cards and have the student read them. Explain that these prefixes can be added to words (at the beginning of a word rather than at the end of a word). Write the word **open** on an index card and have the student read the word. Add the prefix card **re** to make the word **reopen**. Ask the student to point to the baseword then to the prefix. Explain the meaning of the prefix **re**- (to do again). Tell the student that whenever these prefixes are added to basewords that begin with a vowel, the word will divide between the vowels. Make additional examples with the other prefixes. Be sure to discuss the meaning of each prefix as it is used in the words.

Notebook Entry

(Syllable Section) The student should add the exception to the "D" syllable to his notebook.

Follow the procedures for Parts 3, 4, 5, and 6.

 Use Syllable Cards to present 12.1 words to the student. Turn the syllables face down. Say the word and have the student repeat the word, then name and spell one syllable at a time. A dictionary or spell checker can be used as needed to check spelling.

   Follow the procedures for Parts 8, 9, and 10.

 Notes / FYI

Suffixes usually change a word's **part of speech** whereas prefixes change a word's **meaning**. Prefixes have specific meaning. These should be discussed as words are presented. Vocabulary words can be added to the student's notebook to help him learn the meaning of specific prefixes.

 Weave with Questions

"Where is this word divided?"

The two syllables can be identified as exceptions to the "D" syllable:

crē āte
 o   e

12.2 What to Teach

- The silent letter combinations: **gh**, **rh**, **kn**, **gn**, **wr**, **mb**, **mn**

- How to read and spell words with the above combinations

Additional Materials Needed
- 12.2 Syllable Cards, 12.2 Word Cards

 PART 1

Omit Part 1 in the first lesson until after Part 2. Then, present silent letter combination using 2 Sound Cards.

Notebook Entry

(Sound Section) The student should add the silent letter combinations to the additional sounds page in his notebook.

 PART 2

Make the word **ghost** with the Sound Cards.

Read the word (or have the student read it if he knows it). Tell him that one letter in that word is silent. Ask him to repeat the word, tap it out and determine which letter is silent (**h**). Cover the **h** with the blank consonant card g ⬚ ost and reread the word. Explain that certain letters are silent when combined with other letters. Present the following combinations with the individual Sound Cards. Say the letters, cover the silent one and have the student say the remaining sound. For example, present:

r h - cover **h**, and say /**r**/

k n - cover **k**, and say /**n**/

Next, make words with Sound Cards. Have the student locate the silent letter, cover it with the blank consonant card and decode it.

Notebook Entry

(Sound Section) The student should add the spelling options for the sounds /**g**/, /**r**/, /**n**/, and /**m**/ in his sound section.

 PART 3   **PART 4**   **PART 5**   **PART 6**

Follow the procedures for Parts 3, 4, 5, and 6.

PART 7 Make silent letter combinations with Sound Cards and review the sounds. Tell the student that words with silent letters are very tricky to spell since one letter is silent. These words will need to be learned by memory or with repeated exposure and experience. To practice them, dictate a word and have the student repeat the word. He should spell the word using the Sound Cards. For example, say the word **thumb** and have the student repeat and find the cards for the sounds that he hears and then add the silent letter.

Notebook Entry

(Sound Section) The student should add the silent letter combinations to the spelling options for sounds.

 PART 8   **PART 9**   **PART 10** Follow the procedures for Parts 8, 9, and 10.

 Notes / FYI

Several words with silent letters have corresponding homophones. These are especially difficult for spelling. Explain this to the student and discuss the need to check meaning for the correct spelling.

Examples:

write - right

wrap - rap

know - no

knew - new

knight - night

 Weave with Questions

Cross out the silent letter in this word:

gh̸ost

"Which letter in this word is silent?"

12.3 What to Teach

- How /**w**/ affects vowels: **wa**, **war**, **wor**

- How to read and spell words with /**w**/ followed by **a**, **ar**, and **or**

Additional Materials Needed
- 12.3 Syllable Cards, 12.3 Word Cards

PART 1

a

On the first lesson, omit the new sounds for **a**, **ar**, and **or**. After Part 2 and in subsequent lessons, present the Sound Cards and have the student repeat:

a - **apple** - /ă/

a - **safe** - /ā/

a - **acorn** - /ā/

a - **Alaska** - /ə/

a - **wash** - /ȯ/

a - **squash** - /ȯ/

ar - **car** - /ar/

ar - **beggar** - /ər/

ar - **warm** - /or/

or - **horn** - /or/

or - **doctor** - /ər/

or - **worm** - /ər/

PART 2

Explain that the sound /**w**/ effects some vowel sounds. Make the word **wash** with the Sound Cards. Ask the student to name the expected sound of the letter **a** (/ă/). Tell him that /**w**/ often changes the sound of **a** to /ȯ/. Tap out and read **wash**. Have the student listen to the sound of the **a**. Next, make the word **squash** with the Sound Cards. Ask the student what sound **qu** makes /**kw**/. Write down **kw**. Show the student that the **qu** ends with a **w** sound. Due to this, **qu** has the same effect on the letter **a**.

Next, tell the student that /**w**/ effects **ar** and **or** as well. Make the words **warn** and **work**. Discuss the **ar** /or/ and **or** /ər/ sounds in these words. Make additional words with Sound Cards and Syllable Cards. Have the student name the vowel sound and decode the word.

Follow the procedures for Parts 3, 4, and 5.

PART 3 **PART 4** **PART 5**

  Ask "What says /**or**/?" The student should select **or** and **ar** cards.

PART 6

"When does **ar** say /**or**/?" (after /**w**/)

Ask, What says /**ȯ**/? The student should select **au**, **aw** and **a** cards.

"When does **a** say /**ȯ**/?" (after /**w**/)

Ask, "What says /**ər**/?" The student should find **er**, **ir**, **ur**, **ar** and **or** cards.

"When does **or** say /**ər**/?" (At the end of a word or after /**w**/)

Notebook Entry
(Sound Section) The student should add the spelling options for /**ȯ**/, /**or**/, and /**ər**/ to the sound section.

 Dictate 12.3 words. The student should repeat the word and use Sound Cards to spell it. Syllable Cards can be used for multisyllabic words.

PART 7

   Follow the procedures for Parts 8, 9, and 10.

PART 8 **PART 9** **PART 10**

Weave with Questions
"What sounds effect **a**, **ar**, and **or**?" (/**w**/)

"What does **a** say after /**w**/?"

"What does **ar** say after /**w**/?"

"What does **or** say after /**w**/?"

The student can write the sound above the vowel(s) to reinforce:

/ȯ/
wash

12.4   What to Teach

- The /**k**/ sound of **ch**
- The /**k**/ sound of **que** at the end of words (advanced students)
- How to read and spell words with /**k**/

Additional Materials Needed
- 12.4 Syllable Cards, 12.4 Word Cards
- Sound Card **que**

 PART 1

Present the **ch** digraph and ask the student to name its sound /**ch**/. Tell him that it has another sound - /**k**/. Say the letters-keywords-sounds and have the student repeat:

 ch - **chin** - /**ch**/

 ch - **chorus** - /**k**/

Advanced Students

Tell the student that there is another way to spell the sound /**k**/. Present the **que** Sound Card. Tell the student that this says /**k**/ at the end of words. Name the letters-keyword-sound and have the student repeat:

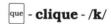 que - **clique** - /**k**/

Notebook Entry

(Sound Section) The /**k**/ sound of **ch** and (advanced students) the **que** must be added to the sound section of the student's notebook.

 PART 2

Make words with **ch** says /**k**/ using Sound Cards or Syllable Cards. Have the student name the sound of **ch** (/**k**/) and decode the word.

Advanced Students

Make word with **que** using the Sound Cards. Make words with **ique** and explain that the letter **i** says /ē/ in words such as **oblique**, **technique**, etc. It helps to replace the **que** (or cover it) with the **k** card to practice decoding these words.

PART 3   **PART 4**   **PART 5**   Follow the procedures for Parts 3, 4, and 5.

PART 6   Ask "What says /**k**/?" The student should find the following cards:

[k]   [c]   [ck]   [ch]   [que] (advanced students)

Notebook Entry

(Sound Section) The student should add the spelling options for /**k**/ to his sound section.

PART 7   Keep the above cards displayed. Dictate various words with the sound of /**k**/. Have the student determine the correct option. Explain that the **ch** says /**k**/ in words that are from the Greek language. Many of these are scientific, medical or musical words. The dictionary or spell checker should be used to determine the correct option

PART 8   **PART 9**   **PART 10**   Follow the procedures for Parts 8, 9, and 10.

Weave with Questions

"What does **ch** say in this word?"

"What says /**k**/ in this word?"

12.5 What to Teach

- The sound of **tu** and **ture**
- The sound of **ti** and **ci** when followed by a suffix (advanced students)
- How to read and spell words with the above sounds

Additional Materials Needed
- Sound Cards **ti**, **ci**, **tu**, and **ture**
- 12.5 Syllable Cards, 12.5 Word Cards

 PART 1 In the first lesson, do not include new Sound Cards in the quick drill. After Part 2, present these Sound Cards and say the letter names, keywords and sounds. The student repeats:

 - **spatula** - /**chü**/    - **capture** - /**chər**/

 - **patient** - /**sh**/   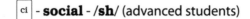 - **social** - /**sh**/ (advanced students)

Notebook Entry
(Sound Section) The student should add the new sounds to the Additional Sounds page of his notebook.

 PART 2 Explain that **ture** says /**chər**/. Make the word pasture with the Sound Cards. Read this to the student and have him repeat it. Ask him to say the sound of **ture** (/**chər**/). Make additional words for the student to decode. Next, tell the student that **tu** says /**chü**/. Make the word **actual**. Use the **tu** Sound Card. Ask, "What does the **tu** say?" (/**chü**/) after the student reads the word, make additional words to practice decoding.

Advanced Students
Explain that **ti** and **ci** say /**sh**/ when followed by a suffix. Make the word:

 (use -**al** Suffix Card)

The **i** connects the root to the suffix. The suffix is part of the word and when removed, **soci** is not a word by itself. This is similar to the **i** connective in Step 11.3. Use Sound Cards and Suffix Cards to make these words. Initially, the student may cover the **ci** or **ti** with the **sh** card to help with decoding.

 PART 3   **PART 4**   **PART 5**   Follow the procedures for Parts 3, 4, and 5.

 PART 6 Ask, "What says /**chər**/?"

"What says /**chü**/?"

When you ask, "What says /**sh**/?", advanced students should answer, "**sh**, **ci**, and **ti**" (before a suffix)

PART 7 Put the green cards **tu** and **ture** on the table or magnetic board. Use Syllable Cards with **tu** and **ture** words such as **pasture**. Turn the cards over, face down. Dictate the word, "**pasture**".

Have the student repeat the word in syllables as he points to the cards. Next, have him place the green Sound Card (**ture**) on the correct Syllable Card. He should then name and spell one syllable at a time and turn the Syllable Cards over and check the spelling.

Advanced Students

Place the **ti** and **ci** consonant cards on the table or magnetic board. Next, have the student place the vowel Suffix Cards. Dictate a word, such as **partial**. Have the student repeat the word in syllables and select blank Syllable Cards to represent the number of syllables in the word.

Next, have the student determine which syllable has the /**sh**/ sound followed by a vowel suffix. Have the student place the suffix on the Syllable Card, as well as the two options for /**sh**/ (**ti** and **ci**).

Have him spell the word by syllable and determine the correct spelling (**ti** or **ci**) by using a dictionary or spell checker. Explain that the **i** connects the root to the suffix. The student should try to recognize a root or word that ends in **t** or **c** to help in choosing. The word **partial**, for example, comes from the word **part** -**i** connective -**al** suffix. Other examples include:

financial   (**finance**)

spacious   (**space**)

racial   (**race**)

The root is not always as clear as in these examples.

PART 8 **PART 9** **PART 10**   Follow the procedures for Parts 8, 9, and 10.

Weave with Questions
"What letters say /**chü**/ in this word?"

"What letters say /**chər**/ in this word?"

Advanced Students
"What letters say /**sh**/ in this word?"

"What is the purpose of the **i**?"

"What is the suffix?"

"Do you recognize a root or baseword?"

12.6 What to Teach

- Some prefixes are added to words that stand alone. Sometimes prefixes are added to Latin roots that have meaning but do not stand alone.

- Some prefixes (called chameleon prefixes) change to match the next letter in the word

- How to read and spell words with chameleon prefixes

Additional Materials Needed
- 12.6 Syllable Cards, 12.6 Word Cards

- Blank index cards

PART 1

Follow the procedure for Part 1.

PART 2

Make the word **reopen** and ask the student to point to and read the prefix. Make the word **nerve** with the Sound Cards and have the student read the word. Write **un** on a blank index card and add it to make the word to make **unnerve**. Have the student point to and read the prefix. Point out that the prefix ends in the letter **n** and the baseword begins with **n**. Thus, the word has a double consonant (one from the prefix and one from the baseword). Whenever a prefix ends in the same consonant that the baseword begins with, the consonant will be doubled. Other examples include **unnecessary**, **misspell** and **disservice**.

Explain that some prefixes attach to word parts, called roots. Write **mit** on an index card, and have the student read this syllable. Explain that **mit** is not a word but it is something called a 'root' and it comes from the Latin language. Explain that **mit** means *send*. Ask if the student can think of any words with **mit** (**admit**, **submit**, **commit**, etc.).

Write the prefixes **trans-**, **ad-**, **sub-**, **com-**, **o-**, and **re-** on index cards. Add these to the **mit** card to make the words. Explain that **trans-**, **ad-**, **sub-**, **com-**, **o-**, and **re-** are actually all prefixes added to the root **mit**. Even though **mit** does not stand alone as a word, it is a Latin root that has meaning. The prefixes further determine the meaning.

Next, present 12.6 words to the student with the Syllable Cards. Have the student locate the prefix in each word. Separate the prefix from the rest of the word. Explain that some prefixes change to match the root. Since they **change**, they can be called chameleon prefixes. Make **cor-**, **col-**, **com-**, and **con-** prefix cards on blank index cards. **Cor**, **col**, **com** all belong to the 'con' family of prefixes meaning *with* or *together*. The **n** in **con** might change to match the root.

correct   **col**lect   **com**mit

Notebook Entry
(Spelling Section) The student can add the list of chameleon prefixes to his notebook. The list is found in the Appendix of this manual and can be photocopied for the student.

PART 3   **PART 4**   **PART 5**   **PART 6**   Follow the procedures for Parts 3, 4, 5, and 6.

PART 7 Explain that each word you will dictate will have two similar consonants - one ending the prefix and one beginning either a word or Latin root. Dictate **collect** and have the student pull down a blank index card for each syllable. He should name and spell one syllable at a time. Be sure the consonant is doubled, even though only one consonant can be heard (it is usually sounded in the stressed root rather than the prefix). Dictate additional 12.6 words to spell the word one syllable at a time.

PART 8   **PART 9**   **PART 10**   Follow the procedures for Parts 8, 9, and 10.

 Notes / FYI

The study of chameleon prefixes and Latin roots can be extensive. The student completing Step 12 can continue the study of the English language in order to increase vocabulary and spelling skills. See the Appendix for a list of chameleon prefixes and source suggestions for further study.

 Weave with Questions

The student can highlight or box the prefixes in the 12.6 words.

APPENDIX

Limited permission is granted to the purchasing party to photocopy ONLY those pages of this Appendix that bear the notice "Permission to photocopy granted" for use with his or her student during their Wilson program. Otherwise, no part of this work may be reproduced or transmitted in any form or by any means, electronic or mechanical, including photocopying, recording, or by information storage and retrieval system or network, without the express permission in writing from Wilson Language Training Corporation.

Wilson Reading System Overview / Scope and Sequence of Word Structure

Step 1   Closed Syllables (3 Sounds)

1.1   **f, l, m, n, r, s,** (initial) and **d, g, p, t,** (final) **a, i, o** (Blending of 2 and 3 sounds)

1.2   **b, sh | u | h, j | c, k, ck | e | v, w, x, y, z | ch, th | qu, wh** (Introduced gradually)

1.3   Practice with above sounds (**wish, chop, wet**)

1.4   Double consonants, **all** (**bill, kiss, call**)

1.5   **am, an** (**ham, fan**)

1.6   Adding suffix -**s** to closed syllable words with 3 sounds (**bugs, chills**)

Step 2   Closed Syllables (4-6 Sounds)

2.1   **ang, ing, ong, ung, ank, ink, onk, unk** (**bang, pink**)

2.2   Closed syllables with blends: 4 sounds only + suffix -**s** (**bled, past, steps**)

2.3   Closed syllable exceptions: **ind, ild, old, ost, olt** (**mold, host**)

2.4   Five sounds in a closed syllable + suffix -**s** (**blend, trumps**)

2.5   Three-letter blends and up to 6 sounds in a closed syllable (**sprint, scrap**)

Step 3   Closed Syllables (Multisyllabic Words)

3.1   Two-syllable words with 2 closed syllables combined - no blends, schwa (**catnip, wagon**)

3.2   Two-syllable words with 2 closed syllables, including blends (**disrupt, fragment**)

3.3   Words with 2 closed syllables ending in **ct** blend (**contract, district**)

3.4   Multisyllabic words, combining only closed syllables (**Wisconsin, establish**)

3.5   -**ed**, -**ing** suffixes added to unchanging basewords with closed syllables (**slashing, blended**)

Step 4   Vowel-Consonant-e Syllable

4.1   Vowel-consonant-e syllable in one-syllable words (**hope, cave**)

4.2   Vowel-consonant-e syllable combined with closed syllables (**combine, reptile**)

4.3   Multisyllabic words combining 2 syllable types (**compensate, illustrate**)

4.4   **ive** exception: no word ends in **v** (**olive, pensive**)

Step 5   Open Syllable

5.1   Open syllable in one-syllable words, **y** as a vowel (**he, hi, shy**)

5.2   Open syllables combined with vowel-consonant-e and closed syllables in two-syllable words (**protect, decline**)

5.3   **y** as a vowel at the end of two-syllable words when combined with a closed syllable or another open syllable (**handy, pony**)

5.4   Multisyllabic words, combining 3 syllable types: open, closed, vowel-consonant-e (**instrument, amputate**)

5.5   **a** and **i** in unaccented, open syllables (**Alaska, indicate**)

Step 6   Suffix Endings (Unchanging Basewords) and Consonant-le Syllable

6.1   Suffix endings -**er**, -**est**, -**en**, -**es**, -**able**, -**ish**, -**y**, -**ive**, -**ly**, -**ty**, -**less**, -**ness**, -**ment**, -**ful** added to unchanging basewords (**thankful, classy**)

6.2   Suffix ending -**ed** (/**d**/, /**t**/) added to unchanging basewords (**thrilled, punished**)

6.3   Combining 2 suffixes to an unchanging baseword (**constructively, helpfulness**)

6.4   Stable final syllable: consonant-le, **stle** exception (**dribble, whistle**)

Wilson Reading System®

Step 7   Introduction to Sound Options, Contractions

7.1 Sound options: **c** {**e**, **i**, **y**} (**concentrate**, **concede**) **g** {**e**, **i**, **y**} (**gentle**, **pungent**)

7.2 **ge**, **ce**, **dge** (**lunge**, **indulgence**, **fudge**)

7.3 New trigraph and digraph: **tch**, **ph** (**fetch**, **pamphlet**)

7.4 **tion**, **sion** (**subtraction**, **expansion**)

7.5 contractions (**we've**, **I'll**)

Step 8   R-Controlled Syllable

8.1 R-controlled syllable: **ar**, **er**, **ir**, **or**, **ur** in one-syllable words (**firm**, **turn**, **barn**)

8.2 **ar**, **or** in multisyllabic words (**market**, **cortex**)

8.3 **er**, **ir**, **ur** in multisyllabic words (**skirmish**, **surgery**)

8.4 Exceptions: vowel **rr** (**hurry**, **barren**), **para**

8.5 Exceptions: **ar**, **or** in final syllable (**beggar**, **doctor**), **ard ward** (**blizzard**, **onward**)

Step 9   Vowel Digraph/Diphthong "D" Syllable

9.1 **ai**, **ay** (**plain**, **display**)

9.2 **ee**, **ey** (**tweezer**, **valley**)

9.3 **oa**, **oe**, **ue** (**croak**, **toe**, **revenue**)

9.4 **oi**, **oy**, **au**, **aw** (**thyroid**, **employ**, **saucer**, **squawk**)

9.5 **ou**, **ow**, **oo** (**trousers**, **drowsy**, **spoon**)

9.6 **ea** (**eat**, **bread**, **steak**)

9.7 **eu**, **ew**, **ui** (**Europe**, **few**, **suit**)

Step 10   Adding Suffixes to Changing Basewords

10.1 v-e exceptions: **ice**, **ace**, **age**, **ate**, **ile**, **ite**, **ine**

10.2 Spelling Rule: Adding a suffix to a baseword ending in **e** (**taping**, **lately**)

10.3 Spelling Rule: Adding a suffix to a one-syllable closed or r-controlled baseword (**starred** or **shopful**)

10.4 Spelling Rule: Adding a suffix to a multisyllabic baseword when the final consonant must double (**regretting**, **controlled**)

10.5 Additional suffixes: -ic, -al, -ible, -ous, -ist, -ism, -ity, -ize, -ary, -ery, -ory, -ent, -ence, -ant, -ance

Step 11   Additional I, E, Y Vowel Work

11.1 **y** in open, closed, v-e syllables (**reply**, **gym**, **type**)

11.2 The **y** spelling rule (**enjoyable**, **player**)

11.3 **i** in an open syllable /ē/ (**orient**), **i** pronounced as /**y**/ (**genius**, **million**)

11.4 **ie** / **ei** (**piece**, **ceiling**, **vein**)

11.5 **igh**, **eigh** (**light**, **eight**)

Step 12   Advanced Concepts

12.1 Split vowels: vowel team exceptions (**create**, **violin**)

12.2 Silent letters: **rh**, **gh**, **mb**, **mn**, **kn**, **gn**, **wr** (**rhyme**, **ghost**, **lamb**, **column**, **knife**, **gnat**, **wrist**)

12.3 **w** effecting vowels (**water**, **worship**)

12.4 **ch**, **que** /k/ (**chorus**, **clique**)

12.5 **ti**, **ci**, **tu**, **ture** (**patient**, **official**, **actual**, **torture**)

12.6 Chameleon prefixes (**correct**, **accent**)

WRS Lesson Plan

DATE	
LESSON NUMBER	
STUDENT NAME / GROUP	

SUBSTEP

LESSON FOCUS
- ☐ INTRODUCTION
- ☐ ACCURACY
- ☐ FLUENCY

CONCEPTS TO WEAVE

WORD TYPE
- ☐ REAL ☐ NONSENSE

"TROUBLE SPOTS"

BLOCK 1 · Word Study

1 SOUND CARDS QUICK DRILL
1:1 ⏱ **2-3 MINUTES**   GROUP ⏱ **2-3 MINUTES**

VOWELS

CONSONANTS

WELDED

_____   _____   _____

_____   _____   _____

ADD TO NOTEBOOK

DRILL LEADER (IF GROUP)

_____   _____

2 TEACH & REVIEW CONCEPTS FOR READING
1:1 ⏱ **5 MINUTES**   GROUP ⏱ **5 MINUTES**

REVIEW CONCEPTS	REVIEW WORDS	CURRENT CONCEPTS	CURRENT WORDS

ADD TO NOTEBOOK

3 WORD CARDS
1:1 ⏱ **3-5 MINUTES**   GROUP ⏱ **5-10 MINUTES**

SUBSTEPS   **ACTIVITY**

VOCABULARY WORDS   *ADD NEW TO NOTEBOOK* ☐

HIGH FREQUENCY / SIGHT WORDS   *ADD NEW TO NOTEBOOK* ☐

4 WORDLIST READING
1:1 ⏱ **5 MINUTES**   GROUP ⏱ **5-10 MINUTES**

STUDENT READER
- ☐ A ☐ B
- ☐ REAL ☐ NONSENSE

PRACTICE
PAGE _____
- ☐ TOP ☐ BOTTOM

CHARTING
PAGE _____
- ☐ TOP ☐ BOTTOM

ERRORS

ACTIVITY (IF GROUP)

WRS LESSON PLAN (060206)

5 SENTENCE READING
1:1 ⏱ **5 MINUTES**   GROUP ⏱ **5 MINUTES**

STUDENT READER
- ☐ A ☐ B

PAGE _____

ERRORS

NOTES

| WRS LESSON PLAN (060206)

BLOCK 2 · Spelling

6 QUICK DRILL IN REVERSE   1:1 ⏲ **1-2 MINUTES**   GROUP ⏲ **2-3 MINUTES**

VOWELS   CONSONANTS   WELDED

_____   _____   _____

_____   _____   _____

7 TEACH & REVIEW CONCEPTS FOR SPELLING   1:1 ⏲ **5 MINUTES**   GROUP ⏲ **5-10 MINUTES**

REVIEW CONCEPTS	REVIEW WORDS	CURRENT CONCEPTS	CURRENT WORDS	HIGH FREQUENCY / SIGHT WORDS
_____	_____	_____	_____	_____
_____	_____	_____	_____	_____
_____	_____	_____	_____	_____
_____		_____	_____	
_____		_____	_____	

ADD TO NOTEBOOK

_____

8 WRITTEN WORK DICTATION (SOUNDS, WORDS, SENTENCES)   1:1 ⏲ **15 MINUTES**   GROUP ⏲ **15-20 MINUTES**

SOUNDS	REAL WORDS	NONSENSE WORDS	HIGH FREQUENCY / SIGHT WORDS
_____	_____	_____	_____
_____	_____	_____	_____
_____	_____	_____	_____
_____	_____	_____	_____

SENTENCES

_____

_____

_____

BLOCK 3 · Fluency / Comprehension

9 CONTROLLED TEXT PASSAGE READING   1:1 ⏲ **10-15 MINUTES**   GROUP ⏲ **10-15 MINUTES**

BOOK   READER LEVEL   VOCABULARY

☐ STUDENT READER _____   ☐ A   ☐ B   _____

☐ STORIES FOR OLDER STUDENTS _____   PAGE(S)   _____

☐ TRAVELS WITH TED   _____   NOTES

☐ WRS FLUENCY READER   _____   _____

10 LISTENING COMPREHENSION / APPLIED SKILLS   1:1 ⏲ **15-30 MINUTES**   GROUP ⏲ **15-30 MINUTES**

PASSAGE FOR LISTENING COMPREHENSION   VOCABULARY

_____   _____

DECODABLE TEXT PASSAGE FOR APPLIED SKILLS   NOTES

_____   _____

WRS Wordlist Chart

Wilson Reading System®

STUDENT NAME

WORD TYPE

R = REAL WORDS   **N** = NONSENSE WORDS

DATE													
SUBSTEP													
WORD TYPE	☐ R ☐ N	☐ R ☐ N	☐ R ☐ N	☐ R ☐ N	☐ R ☐ N	☐ R ☐ N	☐ R ☐ N	☐ R ☐ N	☐ R ☐ N	☐ R ☐ N	☐ R ☐ N	☐ R ☐ N	☐ R ☐ N
15													
14													
13													
12													
11													
10													
9													
8													
7													
6													
5													
4													

WRS Step Posttesting Lesson Plan

Wilson Reading System®

DATE

STEP

STUDENT NAME / GROUP

Review Prior to Testing

1 | SOUND CARDS QUICK DRILL — INCLUDE ALL FROM CURRENT STEP

VOWELS

CONSONANTS

WELDED

_____

_____

2 | MANIPULATE CARDS — REVIEW EACH SUBSTEP

SUBSTEP	REVIEW CONCEPTS	WORDS TO DEMONSTRATE

3 | WORD CARDS — INCLUDE ALL SUBSTEPS FROM STEP

SUBSTEPS

ACTIVITY

Reading Concepts

4 | CHARTING — USE POSTTEST IN STUDENT READER

READER LEVEL / WORDS   REAL   NONSENSE   ERRORS

☐ A   ☐ B   ____ / 15   ____ / 15

5 | MARK UP — COPY WORDLIST POSTTEST FOR STUDENT TO MARK UP AS DIRECTED

Review Prior to Testing

6 | QUICK DRILL IN REVERSE — INCLUDE ALL FROM CURRENT STEP

VOWELS

CONSONANTS

WELDED

_____

_____

7 | MANIPULATE CARDS — REVIEW EACH SUBSTEP

SUBSTEP	REVIEW CONCEPTS	WORDS TO DEMONSTRATE

Spelling

8 | SPELLING TEST

REAL WORDS (15)

NONSENSE WORDS (5)

Terminology

Consonant: flow of air is obstructed

Vowel: air is less restricted than consonants, "open-mouth" sound

Consonant Digraph: 2 consonants with 1 sound (**wh, ch, sh, th, ck, ph**)

Trigraph: 3 letters with one sound (**dge, tch**)

Blend: 2 or more consonants with separate sounds (**bl, st, str, fr**)

Digraph Blend: a consonant digraph with another consonant making a separate sound (e.g. **shr, thr**)

Vowel Digraph: 2 vowels with one sound (**ee, oo**)

Diphthong: a single speech sound that begins with 1 vowel sound and moves to an other in the same syllable (e.g. **oi, ou**)

Schwa: an unexpected or indistinct vowel sound occurring in an unaccented syllable (**pilot, sentiment**)

High Frequency / Sight Word: word that does not follow rules (must be memorized)

Orthography: the art of writing words with the proper letters according to standard usage (spelling)

Phoneme: smallest unit of **sound** (/**f**/, /**sh**/, etc.)

Grapheme: written form of a phoneme (**ph, f, bb, sh**, etc.) - letters representing one sound

Consonants

voiced	unvoiced (voiceless)
v	**f**
g	**k, c**
	h
	w
j	**ch**
m	
n	
b	**p**
z	**s**
zh	**sh**
d	**t** - sometimes sounds like voiced **d** (**settle, matter**)
th (they)	**th** (thin)

*Vowels are voiced. They are produced by an unobstructed flow of air.

Sound Tapping

Tapping always represents the number of sounds:

Green Cards ("Welded" Sounds)

am, an, all: tap at same time with two fingers (two sounds)

onk, ink, etc: tap at same time with three fingers (three sounds)

ind, ild, old, ost: tap at same time with three fingers (three sounds)

ive: tap at same time with two fingers (two sounds)

All Peach & Ivory Cards

These will get one tap because these are all phonemes.

Chameleon Prefixes

Some prefixes change spelling to match the first letter of the following root word. These are commonly called chameleon prefixes.

For example: **collect** - **con** changes to **col** to link with the root, **lect**. (see step 12.6)

Chameleon prefix families:

ad- to, toward
a- **ac**- **af**- **ag**- **al**- **an**- **ap**- **ar**-

con- with, together
co- **col**- **com**- **cor**-

dis- away
di- **dif**-

en- in, into
em-

ex- out
e- **ec**- **ef**-

in- not, in
il- **im**- **ir**-

ob- (various meanings)
oc- **of**- **op**- **o**-

sub- under
suc- **suf**- **sug**- **sup**- **sum**- **sus**-

syn- with, together
syl- **sym**- **syn**-

Note: Many prefixes have schwa vowels sounds. The prefix is added to the more important, stressed root.

Common Latin Roots that are Closed Syllables

cred	junct	rupt	dict	lect	script	duct
miss	sect	fact	mit	sist	flect	pel
spect	flex	pend	struct	ject	press	tract
fect	fid	fract	min	scrib	sens	spec
strict	tox					

These are mostly verb roots. The part of speech changes with **suffix** additions.

Suffixes

Anglo - Saxon Suffixes	Latin Suffixes	Greek
ed	**able / ible**	**ic**
en	**al**	**ical**
er	**ar / or**	**ist**
es	**ate**	**cal**
est	**ation**	
et	**ative**	
ing	**age**	
ish	**ive**	
y	**ic**	
	ous	
s	**ior**	
ful	**us**	
less	**ure**	
ness	**ment**	
ly	**tion / sion (ion)**	
hood	**ture**	

Resources for Further Word Study

Anderson, C.W., Cross, T., and Stoner, J. *Essential Roots, Prefixes and Suffixes*. Lincoln, NE: Educational Tutorial Consortium, Inc.

Haskell, E. and Rudginsky, L. (1984). *How to Teach Spelling*. Cambridge, MA: Educators Publishing Service, Inc.

Henry, M. K. (1990). *WORDS: Integrated Decoding and Spelling Instruction Based on Word Origin and Word Structure.* Austin, TX: Pro-Ed.

Kleiber, M. (1993). *Specific Language Training - Advanced Level.* Bronx, NY: Decatur Enterprises.

Moats, L. C. (1995). *Spelling Development Disability and Instruction.* Baltimore: York Press.

Rak, Elsie T. (1979). *The Spell of Words.* Cambridge, MA: Educators Publishing Service, Inc.

Wilson, B. A. (2009). *Wilson Just Words® Instructor Manual.* Oxford, MA: Wilson Language Training Corporation.

Wimer, D. (1994). *Word Studies - A Classical Perspective.* Richmond, VA: Print Shack.

Resources

Organizations

Academy of Orton-Gillingham Practitioners and Educators
P.O. Box 234
Amenia, NY 12051-0234
(845) 373-8919 · Fax (845) 373-8925
www.ortonacademy.org

International Dyslexia Association, The
40 York Rd., 4th Floor
Baltimore, MD 21204
(401) 296-0232
www.interdys.org

Learning Disabilities Association of America
4156 Library Road
Pittsburgh, PA 15234-1349
(412) 341-1515
www.ldanatl.org

National Center for Learning Disabilities
381 Park Avenue South, Suite 1401
New York, NY 10016
(212) 545-7510 · Fax (212) 545-9665
www.ncld.org

National Institute for Literacy (NIFL)
1775 I Street NW; Suite 730
Washington, DC 20006-2401
www.nifl.gov

National Institute of Child Health and Human Development (NICHD)
Bldg 31, Room 2A32, MSC 2425
31 Center Drive
Bethesda, MD 20892-2425
www.nichd.nih.gov

Wilson Academy® / Intensive Learning Community

The place to go for Wilson Reading System® online professional learning and support

The Intensive Learning Community of Wilson Academy is a dynamic online resource designed to provide professional learning courses, reference and instructional material, and networking opportunities to the Wilson Reading System teaching community.

The Intensive Learning Community is open to all individuals who have completed the WRS Introductory Workshop within the last five years. (Completion of this prerequisite will be confirmed during the registration process.) New teachers and veteran WRS teachers alike will value the printable materials, additional resources, the idea sharing, and the support.

The Intensive Learning Community membership provides a wealth of WRS resources, including:

- Animated demonstrations from Steps 1-6 such as tapping and marking up
- Printable materials such as student notebook pages, lesson plan tools, extra word cards, fluency practice, and games
- Weekly stories at enriched and non-controlled decodable level for Part 10 of the lesson plan
- Discussion board monitored by a Wilson Literacy Specialist
- Chats led by a Wilson Literacy Specialist

Membership is for a 12-month period, and is renewable annually at no charge.

Assessments

Mather, N., Hammill, D., Allen, E., and Roberts, R. 2004. *Test of Silent Word Reading Fluency (TOSWRF)*. Austin, TX: Pro-Ed Inc.

Torgesen, J. K., and Bryant, B.R. 1984. *Test of Phonological Awareness,* Austin, TX: Pro-Ed Inc.

Wechsler Individual Achievement Test®, Third Edition (WIAT®–III). 2009. San Antonio, TX: Pearson Education.

Wilson, B.A. 1998. *Wilson Assessment of Decoding and Encoding (WADE)*. Oxford, MA: Wilson Language Training.

Wilson, B.A., and Felton, R.H. 2005. *Word Identification and Spelling Test (WIST)* Kit. Austin: Pro-Ed Inc.

Woodcock, R. 1987. *Woodcock Reading Mastery Tests-Revised*. Circle Pines, MN: American Guidance.

Woodcock, R., and Mather, N. 1989. *Woodcock - Johnson Tests of Achievement*. Allen, TX: DLM.

Woodcock, R., Mather, N., and Schrank, F.A. 2004. *Woodcock-Johnson® III Diagnostic Reading Battery (WJ III® DRB)*. Rolling Meadows, IL: Riverside Publishing.

Resources

Controlled Text

For Elementary Grades

Younger students with A level vocabulary can use the following controlled material to get additional practice reading:

BurnsBooks Publishing
Chapter books for dyslexic and beginning readers
(203) 744-0232
www.burnsbookspublishing.com

Flyleaf Publishing
Decodable readers
(800) 449-7006
www.flyleafpublishing.com

Vangar Publishers
Short vowel chapter books
(304) 728-2829
www.vangarpublishers.com

Wilson Language Training
No Fish! Decodable Poems
(800) 899-8454
www.wilsonlanguage.com

For Students Beyond Elementary Grades

Students beyond the elementary grades can use the following controlled material to get additional practice reading:

Sopris West
J & J Language Readers
(303) 651-2829 or (800) 547-6747
www.soprieswest.com

Wilson Language Training
Wilson Academy® / Intensive Learning Community online resource: Paired enriched and non-controlled decodable text passages
(800) 899-8454
www.wilsonacademy.com

Fluency Resources

Wilson Language Training
Wilson Fluency® / Basic by Barbara A. Wilson
(800) 899-8454
www.wilsonlanguage.com
WILSON Fluency / Basic is designed to provide explicit fluency instruction and reading practice to develop the application of skills with connected text.

Great Leaps
(877) 475-3277
www.greatleaps.com

Read Naturally®
(651) 452-4085
www.readnaturally.com

Sopris West
The Six Minute Solution: A reading fluency program by Gail Adams and Sheron Brown
(303) 651-2829 or (800) 547-6747
www.sopriswest.com

Vocabulary Resources

Beck, I.L., Kucan, L., and McKeown, M.G. (2002). *Bringing words to life: Robust vocabulary instruction.* New York: The Guilford Press.

Collins Cobuild new learners dictionary (2nd ed.). 2003. Great Britain: HarperCollins.

Henry, M. (2003). *Unlocking literacy: Effective decoding and spelling instruction.* Baltimore: Brookes Publishing.

Lehr, F. Osborn, J. Hiebert, E. H. *A focus on vocabulary.* Research-Based Practices in Early Reading Series. www.prel.org/products/re_/ES0419.htm

The unofficial SAT word dictionary. (2002). Punta Gorda, FL: New Monic Books.

Comprehension Strategies

Wilson Comprehension S.O.S.™

Reading for meaning typically entails forming images of the content in the "mind's eye." A student with a language-based learning disability may not be able to do this. Wilson Comprehension S.O.S.™ — Stop, Orient, Scaffold/Support — is a strategy for guiding students to create an image or "make a movie" of the text passage as they read.

Comprehension S.O.S. is used during the reading comprehension part of the Wilson lesson. The teacher reads a text passage to student(s), and has the student(s) replay (imagine) and retell it in his or her own words. If a student's retelling is scanty and devoid of detail, Comprehension S.O.S. is called for.

Remember that the process is not an exact science, but more of a "dance." If you achieve a balance between eliciting students' understanding and providing explanations, you'll find your students' listening comprehension will improve considerably.

Handwriting

Programs based upon Orton-Gillingham philosophy stress cursive handwriting. Cursive helps eliminate reversals and aids in fluency of writing. The following programs are recommended to teach cursive:

Wilson Cursive® Writing Kit by Barbara A. Wilson
Wilson Language Training
(800) 899-8454
www.wilsonlanguage.com

Cursive Writing Skills (2nd Edition) by Diana Hanbury King
Educators Publishing Service
(800) 225-5750
www.intervention.schoolspecialty.com

If teaching an elementary grade student, it is well worth all the time and effort. Correct motor patterns can be developed before bad habits are in place.

Most students beyond elementary grades have firmly established motor patterns. Students beyond elementary grades can establish new patterns, but this takes extensive time and effort. If your teaching time with a student is limited, it is best to direct it toward reading and spelling. The student can be taught how to write as neatly as possible with some time spent improving specific letter formations. If a student is in a program that has enough time to devote to handwriting, as well as the reading and spelling, new patterns can be established. Most often, however, this is not the case. It is most important, then to teach keyboarding skills. This should be done with *Keyboarding Skills* by Diana Hanbury King from Educators Publishing Service in Cambridge, MA.

Additional Resources

The Pencil Grip
(888) 736-4747
www.thepencilgrip.com

The Pencil Grip is a small tool that, when placed on a pencil, places fingers in the proper position for gripping.

Acknowledgment of Completion

_____

has made excellent progress through Step _____ in the

WILSON READING SYSTEM®

_____

Date

_____   _____
Wilson Language Trainer   Teacher

Upon student completion of all WRS 12 Steps, contact info@wilsonlanguage.com to request a Certificate of Achievement.

Wilson Reading System®

References and Further Reading

Achieve, Inc. (2005). *Rising to the challenge: Are high school graduates prepared for college and work?* Washington, DC: Author.

Alexander-Passe, N. (2008). Sources and manifestations of stress amongst school-aged dyslexics, compared with sibling controls. Dyslexia, 14(4), 291-313. doi:10.1002/dys.351

Alvermann, D., & Moore, D. (1991). Secondary school reading. In R. Barr, M. Kamil, P. Mosenthal, & P.D. Pearson (Eds.), *Handbook of Reading Research, 2,* 1013-46. New York: Longman, Inc.

Alvermann, D.E. (2001). *Effective literacy instruction for adolescents.* Executive Summary and Paper Commissioned by the National Reading Conference. Chicago, IL: National Reading Conference.

American Federation of Teachers. (1999). *Teaching reading is rocket science: What expert teachers of reading should know and be able to do.* Washington, DC: Author.

Anderson, R.C., Wilkinson, I.A.G., & Mason, J.M. (1991). A microanalysis of the small-group, guided reading lesson: Effects of an emphasis on global story meaning. *Reading Research Quarterly, 26,* 417-441.

Anderson, R.C., Wilson, P.T., & Fielding, L.G. (1988). Growth in reading and how children spend their time outside of school. *Reading Research Quarterly, 23,* 285-303, 611-626.

August, D., Carlo, M., Dressler, C., & Snow, C. (2005). The critical role of vocabulary development for English language learners. *Learning Disabilities: Research and Practice 20(I),* pp. 50-57

August, D., & Shanahan, T. (Eds.). (2006). *Developing literacy in second-language learners: Report of the National Literacy Panel on Language-Minority Children and Youth.* London: Lawrence Erlbaum Associates.

Author not credited. (2006). *Why the crisis in adolescent literacy demands a national response.* Washington, DC: Alliance for Excellent Education.

Ball, E.W. (1993). Phonological awareness: What's important and to whom? *Reading and Writing: An Interdisciplinary Journal, 5,* 141-59.

Balmuth, Miriam. (1992). *Roots of phonics.* Baltimore: York Press.

Banks, S.R., Guyer, B.P., & Guyer, K.E. (1993). Spelling improvement by college students who are dyslexic. *Annals of Dyslexia 43,* 186-93.

Bernhardt, E. (2005). Progress and procrastination in second language reading. *Annual Review of Applied Linguistics, 25,* 133-150.

Bhattacharya, A., & Ehri, L.C. (2004). Graphosyllabic analysis helps adolescent struggling readers read and spell words. *Journal of Learning Disabilities, 37(4),* 331-348.

References and Further Reading (continued)

Biancarosa, C., & Snow, C.E. (2006). *Reading next—A vision for action and research in middle and high school literacy: A report to Carnegie Corporation of New York (2nd ed.)*. Washington, DC: Alliance for Excellent Education.

Birsh, J. (Ed.) (2011). *Multisensory teaching of basic language skills.* Baltimore, MD: Paul H. Brooks Publishing.

Bowler, R. (Ed.). (1987). *Intimacy with language.* Baltimore: Orton Dyslexia Society.

Brady & Shankweiler (Ed.). (1991). *Phonological processes in literacy - A tribute to Isabelle Y. Liberman.* Hillsdale, NJ: Lawrence Erlbaum Associates.

Bruck, M. (1990). Word recognition skill of adults with childhood diagnoses of dyslexia. *Developmental Psychology, 26,* 439-454.

Bruck, M. (1992). Persistence of dyslexics' phonological awareness deficits. *Developmental Psychology, 28,* 874-886.

Bruck, M. (1993). Component spelling skills of college students with childhood diagnoses of dyslexia. *Developmental Psychology, 16,* 171-184.

Bursuck, W., & Dickson, S. (1999). Implementing a model for preventing reading failure: A report from the field. *Learning Disabilities Research & Practice, 14(4),* 191-202. Hillsdale, NJ: Lawrence Erlbaum Associates, Inc.

Bryant, P.E., & Bradley, L. (1983). Psychological strategies and the development of reading and writing. In Martlew, M. (Ed.), *The Psychology of Written Language: Development and Educational Perspectives.* Chichester, UK: Wiley.

Bryson, B. (1990). *Mother tongue: English and how it got that way.* Glencoe: New Press.

Carlisle, J.F., & Fleming, J. (2003). Lexical processing of morphologically complex words in the elementary years. *Scientific Studies of Reading, 7(3),* 239-254.

Carnevale, A.P. (2001). *Help wanted … college required.* Washington, DC: Educational Testing Service, Office for Public Leadership.

Chall, J.S. (1983). *Stages of reading development.* New York: McGraw-Hill.

Chard, D.J., Vaughn, S., & Tyler, B.J. (2002). A synthesis of research on effective interventions for building reading fluency with elementary students with learning disabilities. *Journal of Learning Disabilities, 35,* 386-406.

Childs, S.B. (Ed.). (1968). *Education and specific language disability: The papers of Anna Gillingham.* M.A. 1919-1963. Monograph No. 3. Baltimore: The Orton Society.

References and Further Reading (continued)

Chomsky, C. (1970). Reading, writing and phonology. *Harvard Educational Review, 40*(2): 287-309.

Clark, D., & Uhry, J. (1995.) *Dyslexia: Theory and practice of remedial instruction, revised*. Baltimore, MD: York Press.

Clarke, Louise. (1973). *Can't read, can't write, can't talk too good either*. New York: Penguin Books.

Cordoni, B. (1987). *Living with a learning disability*. Carbondale: Southern Illinois University Press.

Cunningham, A.E., & Stanovich, K.E. (1997). Early reading acquisition and its relation to reading experience and ability 10 years later. *Developmental Psychology, 33,* 934-935.

Curtis, M. (2004). Adolescents who struggle with word identification: Research and practice. In T. Jetton & J. Dole (Eds.), *Adolescent Literacy Research and Practice*. New York: Guilford.

Curtis, M.E. (2002). *Adolescent reading: A synthesis of research*. Boston: Lesley College, The Center for Special Education.

Curtis, M.E., & McCart, L. (1992). Fun ways to promote poor readers' word recognition. *Journal of Reading 35,* 398-99.

Curtis, M.E., & Longo, A.M. (1999). *When adolescents can't read: Methods and materials that work*. Cambridge, MA: Brookline Books.

Daniel, S.S., Walsh, A.K., Goldston, D.B., Arnold, E.M., Reboussin, B.A., & Wood, F.B. (2006). Suicidality, school dropout and reading problems amongst adolescents. *Journal of Learning Disabilities, 39*(6), 507-514.

Denton, C.A., Fletcher, J.M., Anthony, J.L., & Francis, D.J. (2006). An evaluation of intensive intervention for students with persistent reading difficulties. *Journal of Learning Disabilities, 39,* 447-466.

Deshler, D.D., Schumaker, J.B., Lenz, B.K., Bulgren, J.A., Hock, M.F., Knight, J., et al. (2001). Ensuring content-area learning by secondary students with learning disabilities. *Learning Disabilities Research & Practice, 16(2),* 96-108.

Deshler, D.D., Sullivan Palincsar, A., Biancarosa, G., & Nair, M. (2007). *Informed Choices for Struggling Adolescent Readers: A Research-Based Guide to Instructional Programs and Practices*. New York: Carnegie Corporation.

Duane, Drake, & Gray, David B. (eds.). (1991). *The reading brain: The biological basis of dyslexia*. Baltimore: York Press.

Felton, R., & Wilson, B.A. (2004). *Word Identification and Spelling Test (WIST)*. Austin, TX: Pro-Ed.

Ferguson, C., Menn, L. & Stoel-Gammon, C. (Eds.). (1992). *Phonological development - Models, research, implications*. Baltimore: York Press.

References and Further Reading (continued)

Fink, R. (1998). Literacy development in successful men and woman with dyslexia. *Annals of Dyslexia, 48,* 311-346.

Fink, R.P. (1995). Successful dyslexics: A constructive study of passionate interest reading. *Journal of Adolescent & Adult Literacy, 39*(4), 268-280.

Fisher, D., & Ivey, G. (2006). Evaluating the interventions for struggling adolescent readers. *Journal of Adolescent and Adult Literacy, 50,* 180-189.

Fletcher, J.M., Lyon G.R., Fuchs, L.S., & Barnes, M.A. (2007). *Learning disabilities: from identification to intervention.* New York: Guilford Press.

Francis, D.J., Rivera, M., Lesaux, N., Kieffer, M., & Rivera, H. (2006). *Practical guidelines for the education of English language learners: research-based recommendations for instruction and academic interventions.* Houston, Texas: Center on Instruction. Retrieved 1/10/07 from: http://www.centeroninstruction.org/resources.cfm?category=ell&subcategory=research&grade_start=0&grade_end=12, pp.3-30

Frith, U. (1980). Unexpected spelling problems. *Cognitive processes in spelling.* New York: Academic Press.

Genesee, F., Lindholm-Leary, K., Saunders, W., & Christian, D. (Eds.). (2006). *Educating English language learners: A synthesis of research evidence.* New York: Cambridge University Press.

Gerber, M., Jimenez, T., Leafstedt, J. M., Villaruz, J., Richards, C., & English, J. (2004). English reading effects of small-group intensive intervention in Spanish for K–1 English learners. *Learning Disabilities Research Practice, 19*(4), 239–251.

Geschwind, N. (1982). Why Orton was right. *Annals of Dyslexia, 32,* 13-20.

Gillingham, A., & Stillman, B. (1956, 1963, 1977). *Remedial training for children with specific disability in reading, spelling and penmanship.* Cambridge, MA: Educators Publishing Service.

Greene, J.F., & Winters, M. (2005). The effect of school choice on public high school graduation rates. *Education Working Paper.* New York: Manhattan Institute for Public Policy.

Hanna, P.R., Hanna, J.S., Hodges, R.E., & Rudorf, E.H., Jr. (1966). *Phoneme-grapheme correspondences as cues to spelling improvement* (USOE Publication No. 32008). Washington, DC: U.S. Government Printing Office.

Hasbrouck, J.E., & Tindal, G.A. (2006). Oral Reading fluency norms: A valuable assessment tool for reading teachers. *The Reading Teacher, 59*(7), 636-644.

Healy, J. *Your child's growing mind.* New York: Doubleday Books.

Henderson, E. (1990). *Learning to read and spell.* DeKalb, IL: Northern Illinois University Press.

References and Further Reading (continued)

Henry, M. (1988). Beyond phonics; Integrated coding and spelling instruction based on word origin and structure. *Annals of Dyslexia, 38*; 259-275. Baltimore: The Orton Society.

Henry, M.K. (1993). Morphological structure: Latin and Greek roots and affixes as upper grade code strategies. *Reading and Writing: An Interdisciplinary Journal, 5*(2), 227-241.

Henry, M. & Redding, N. (1996). *Patterns for success in reading and spelling.* Austin, TX: Pro-Ed.

Hiebert, E.H. (2002). Standards, assessment, and text difficulty. In A.E. Farstrup and S.J. Samuels (Eds.), *What research has to say about reading instruction, 3,* 337-369. Newark, DE: International Reading Association.

Hiebert, E.H., & Kamil, M. (Eds.). (2005). *Teaching and learning vocabulary: Bringing scientific research to practice.* Mahwah, NJ: Erlbaum.

Higgins, K., Boone, R., & Lovitt, T. (1996). Hypertext support for remedial students and students with learning disabilities. *Journal of Learning Disabilities, 29,*(4), 402-412.

Hirsch, E.D. (2003). Reading comprehension requires knowledge of words and of the world: Scientific insights into fourth-grade slump and stagnant reading comprehension. *American Educator, Spring 2003,* American Federation of Teachers, www.aft.org.

Hirsch, E.D. (2006). *The knowledge deficit.* New York: Houghton Mifflin Company.

Hock, M.F., Deshler, D.D., Marquis, J.G., & Brasseur, I.F. (2005). *Reading component skills of adolescents attending urban schools.* Lawrence: The University of Kansas Center for Research on Learning.

Hock, M.F., Brasseur, I.F., Deshler, D.D., Catts, H.W., Marquis, J.G., Mark, C.A., Stribling, J.W. (2009). What is the reading component skill profile of adolescent struggling readers in urban schools. *Learning Disability Quarterly, 31(1),* 21-38.

Hoffman, P.R., & Norris, J.A. (1989). On the nature of phonological development: Evidence from normal children's spelling errors. *Journal of Speech and Hearing Research, 32,* 787-94.

Homan, S.P., Klesius, J.P., & Hite, C. (1993). Effects of repeated readings and nonrepetitive strategies on students' fluency and comprehension. *Journal of Educational Research, 87,* 94-99.

Hosp, M.K., Hosp, J.L., & Howell, K. W. (2007). *The ABC's of CBM: a practical guide to curriculum-based measurement.* New York: Guilford.

Irvin, J.L., Meltzer, J., & Dukes, M. (2007). Taking action on adolescent literacy: An implementation guide for school leaders. Alexandria, VA: Association for Supervision and Curriculum Development.

Ivey, G., & Broaddus, K. (2001). Just plain reading: A survey of what makes students want to read in middle school classrooms. *Reading Research Quarterly, 36,* 350-377.

References and Further Reading (continued)

Jager-Adams, M. (1990). *Beginning to read.* Cambridge: MIT Press.

Janney, R., & Snell, M. (2000). *Modifying schoolwork (2nd ed.).* Baltimore: Paul H. Brookes Publishing.

Jansky, J., & de Hirsch, K. (1972). *Preventing reading failure - Prediction, diagnosis, intervention.* New York: Harper and Row.

Johnson, Doris, & Blalock, J. (1986). *Young adults with learning disabilities - Clinical studies.* Grune and Stratton.

Joseph, L.M., & Schisler, R. (2009). Should adolescents go back to the basics?: A review of teaching word reading skills to middle and high school students. *Remedial and Special Education, 30* (3), 131-147

Kamhi, A.G., & Catts, H.W. (1989). *Reading disabilities: A developmental language perspective.* Boston: Little, Brown and Co.

Kamil, M. (2003). Adolescents and literacy: reading for the 21st century. Washington, DC: Alliance for Excellent Education.

Kamil, M.L., Intrator, S.M., & Kim, H.S. (2000). The effects of other technologies on literacy and literacy learning. In M.L. Kamil, P.B. Mosenthal, P.D. Pearson, & R. Barr (Eds.), *Handbook of Reading Research 3,* 771-788. Mahwah, NJ: Lawrence Erlbaum.

Kavanagh, J., & Venezky, R. (1980). *Orthography, reading, and dyslexia.* Baltimore: University Park Press.

Kavanagh, J.F., & Truss, T.J. (Eds.). (1988). *Learning disabilities proceedings of the National Conference.* Baltimore: York Press.

Kavanagh, James F. (Ed.). (1991). *The language continuum from infancy to literacy.* Parkton, MD: York Press.

Kim, H., & Kamil, M. (2004). Adolescents, computer technology, and literacy. In T. Jetton & J. Dole (Eds.), *Adolescent Literacy Research and Practice.* New York: Guilford.

Kuhn, M. R., & Stahl, S.A. (2003) Fluency: A review of developmental and remedial practices. *Journal of Educational Psychology 95(I), 3-21.*

Leach, J., Scarborough, H. & Rescorla, L. (2003). Late-emerging reading disabilities. *Journal of Educational Psychology, 95,* 211-224.

Lederer, R. (1991). *The miracle of language.* New York: Pocket Books.

Lieberman, Philip. (1984). *The biology and evolution of language.* Cambridge: Harvard University Press.

Liberman, I.Y. (1993). A language-oriented view of reading and its disabilities in H. Mykelbust (Ed.), *Progress in Learning Disabilities, 5,* 81-101. New York: Grune and Stratton.

Wilson Reading System®

References and Further Reading (continued)

Liberman, I.Y., & Shankweiler, D. (1985). Phonology and the problems of learning to read and write. *Remedial and Special Education, 6*, 8-17.

Lovett, M.W., Barron, R.W., & Benson, N.J. (2003). Effective remediation of word identification and decoding difficulties in school-age children with reading disabilities. In H.L. Swanson, K.R. Harris, & S. Graham (Eds.), *Handbook of Learning Disabilities* (pp. 273-292). New York: Guilford.

Lyon, G.R. (Ed.). (1992). *Frames of reference for the assessment of learning disabilities.* Baltimore: Paul H. Brookes Publishing Co.

Lyon, G.R., Gray, D., Kavanagh, J., & Kasnegor, N. (1993). *Better understanding learning disabilities - New views from research and their implications for education and public policies.* Baltimore: P.H. Brookes Publishing Co.

Lyon, G.R., Fletcher, J.M. Shaywitz, S.E., Shaywitz, B.A., Torgesen, J.K., Wood, F.B., et al. (2001). Rethinking learning disabilities. In C.E. Finn, Jr., A.J. Rotherham, & C.R. Hokanson, Jr. (Eds.), *Rethinking special education for a new century* (pp. 259-287). Washington, DC: Thomas B. Fordham Foundation and Progressive Policy Institute.

Mather, N. and Wendling, B.J. (2012). *Essentials of Dyslexia Assessment and Intervention.* Hoboken, NJ: John Wiley & Sons, Inc.

Mather, N. & Goldstein, S. (2001). *Learning Disabilities and Challenging Behaviors - A Guide to Intervention and Classroom Management.* Baltimore, MD: Brookes Publishing Company.

McCray, A.D. (2001). Middle school students with learning disabilities. *Reading Teacher, 55*(3), 298-310.

McCray, A., Vaughn, S., & Neal, L.I. (2001). Not all students learn to read by third grade: Middle school students speak out about their reading disabilities. *The Journal of Special Education, 35*(1), 17-30. doi:10.1177/002246690103500103

McCutchen, D., Harry, D.R., Cunningham, A.E., Cox, S., Sidman, S., & Covill, A.E. (2002). Reading teachers' knowledge of children's literature and English phonology. *Annals of Dyslexia, 52*, 207-228.

McPeak, L., & Trigg, L. (2007). *The secondary literacy instruction and intervention guide.* Mill Valley, CA: Stupski Foundation.

Moats, L.C. (1998). Reading, spelling and writing disabilities in the middle grades. In Wong, B. (Ed.), *Learning About Learning Disabilities.* Orlando FL: Academic Press.

Moats, L.C. (1995). *Spelling development disability and instruction.* Baltimore: York Press.

Moats, L.C., & Lyon, G.R. (1996). Wanted: Teachers with knowledge of language. *Topics of Language Disorders, 16* (2) 73-86. Apsen Publishers, Inc.

Moore, D.W., Bean, T.W., Birdyshaw, D., & Rycik, J.A. (1999). *Adolescent literacy: A position statement for the Commission on Adolescent Literacy of the International Reading Association.* Newark, DE: International Reading Association.

References and Further Reading (continued)

Nagy, W.E. (1988). *Teaching vocabulary to improve reading comprehension.* Newark, DE: International Reading Association.

Nagy, W.E. & Anderson, R.C. (1984). How many words are there in printed school English? *Reading Research Quarterly, 19,* 304-330.

Nagy, W.E., Diakidoy, I.N., & Anderson, R.C. (1993). The acquisition of morphology: Learning the contribution of suffixes to the meanings of derivatives. *Journal of Reading Behavior, 25,* 155-170.

National Assessment of Educational Progress (NAEP). (2007). Website for NAEP data from 2002. Available at http://nces.ed.gov/nationsreportcard/pdf/main2002/2003521.pdf

National Association of State Boards of Education (NASBE). (2006). Reading at risk: The state response to the crisis in adolescent literacy. Arlington, VA. http://www.instructionalcenter.org/files/Reading_At_Risk_Full_Report.pdf

National Center for Education Statistics (NCES). (2007). National assessment of educational progress/ Nation's report card. Washington, DC: Institute of Education Sciences, U.S. Department of Education. Retrieved 1/25/2008 from http://nces.ed.gov/nationsreportcard/nde/viewresults.asp

National Governors Association (NGA) Center for Best Practices. (2005). Reading to achieve: A governor's guide to adolescent literacy. Washington, DC. Also available online: http://www.nga.org/Files/pdf/0510GOVGUIDELITERACY.PDF

National Institute of Child Health and Human Development (NICHD). (2000). *Report of the National Reading Panel. Teaching children to read: An evidence-based assessment of the scientific research literature on reading and its implications for reading instruction: Reports of the subgroups* (National Institute of health Pub. No. 00-4754). Washington, DC: U.S. Government Printing Office. Also available online: http://www.nichd.nih.gov/publications/nrp/report.htm.

National Literacy Project. (2006). *A resource guide for adolescent literacy; Prepared for the Bill & Melinda Gates Foundation.*

North Central Regional Educational Laboratory. (2005). *Adolescent Literacy Intervention Programs: Chart and program review guide.* (Contract number ED-01-CO-0011).

O'Brien, D.G., Dillon, D.R., Wellinski, S.A., Springs, R., & Stith, D. (1997). *Engaging "at-risk" high school students.* Athens, GA: National Reading Research Center.

O'Connor, J., & Wilson, B. (1995). Effectiveness of the Wilson Reading System used in public school training. In McIntyre & Pickering (Eds.), *Clinical studies of multisensory structured language education for students with dyslexia and related disorders.* Salem, OR: International Multisensory Structured Language Education Council.

Orton, J.L. (1964). *A guide to teaching phonics.* Cambridge: Educators Publishing Service.

References and Further Reading (continued)

Orton, J.L., (Ed.). (1966). "Word-Blindness" in school children and other papers *(Specific Language Disability - Dyslexia)* 1925 - 1946, by Samuel Torrey Orton, M.D. Monograph No. 2. Baltimore: The Orton Society.

Orton, S.T. (1937). *Reading, writing and speech problems in children.* New York: W.W. Norton.

O'Shea, L.J., Sindelar, P.T. & O'Shea, D.J. (1985). The effects of repeated readings and attentional cues on reading fluency and comprehension. *Journal of Reading Behavior, 17,* 129-142.

Paivio, A. (1979). *Imagery and verbal processes.* Hillsdale, NJ: Erlbaum.

The Partnership for Reading. (2003, June). *Put reading first: The research building blocks for teaching children to read. Kindergarten through grade 3* (2nd ed.). Washington, DC: Author. (Available from ED Pubs, 800-228-8813, Post Office Box 1398, Jessup, MD 20794-1398, edpuborders@edpubs.org; also available online: http://www.nifl.gov/paternshipforreading/publications/PFRbookletBW.pdf)

Penney, C. (2002). Teaching decoding skills to poor readers in high school. *Journal of Literacy Research, 34,* 99-118.

Pink, D.H. (2005). *A whole new mind: Moving from the information age to the conceptual age.* New York: Riverhead Books.

Pollard-Durodola, S.D., Mathes, P.G., Vaughn, S., Cardenas-Hagan, E., & Linan-Thompson, S. (2006). The role of oracy in developing comprehension in Spanish-speaking English language learners. *Topics in Language Disorders, 26*(4), 365–384.

RAND Reading Study Group (2002). Reading for understanding: Toward a research and development program in reading comprehension. Santa Monica, CA: RAND Corporation. http://www.rand.org.multi/achievementforall/reading/read report.html.

Rashotte, C.A., & Torgesen, J.K. (1985). Repeated reading and reading fluency in learning disabled children. *Reading Research Quarterly, 20,* 180-188.

Rasinski, T.V., Padak, N.D., McKeon, C.A., Wilfong, L.G., Friedauer, J.A., & Heim, P. (2005). *Is reading fluency a key for successful high school reading? Journal of Adolescent and Adult Literacy, 49*(1), 22-27.

Raskind, M.H., Goldberg, R.J., Higgins, E.L. & Herman, K.L. (1999). Patterns of change and predictors of success in individuals with learning disabilities: Results from a twenty-year longitudinal study. *Learning Disabilities Research& Practice, 14*(1), 35-49.

Read, C. (1971). Pre-school children's knowledge of English phonology. *Harvard Educational Review, 41*, 1-34.

Reiff, H.B., Gerber, P.J., & Ginsberg, R. (1997). *Exceeding expectations: Successful adults with learning disabilities.* Austin, TX: Pro-Ed.

References and Further Reading (continued)

Santa, C.M. (2006). A vision for adolescent literacy: Ours or theirs? *Journal of Adolescent and Adult Literacy, 49*(6), 466-676

Scammacca, N., Roberts, G., Vaughn, S., Edmonds, M., Wexler, J., Reutebuch, C. K., et al. (2007). *Intervention for adolescent struggling readers: A meta-analysis with implications for practice.* Portsmouth, NH: RMC Research Corporation, Center on Instruction.

Schwartz, R. Using phonemic awareness with ESL students. *Linkages*, Washington, D.C.: National ALLD Center.

Semrud-Clikeman, M. (2005). Neuropsychological aspects for evaluating learning disabilities. *Journal of Learning Disabilities, 38*, 563-568.

Shaywitz, S. (2003). *Overcoming dyslexia: A new and complete science-based program for reading problems at any level.* New York: Knopf.

Shaywitz, S.E., Fletcher, J.M., Holahan, J.M., Schneider, A.E., Marchione, K.E., Stuebing, K.K. et al. (1999). Persistence of dyslexia: The Connecticut longitudinal study at adolescence. *Pediatrics, 104(6)*, 1351-1359. doi:10.1542/peds.104.6.1351

Snow, C.E. (2002). *Reading for understanding: Toward an R&D program in reading comprehension.* Santa Monica, CA: Science and Technology Policy Institute. RAND Education.

Snow, C., & Biancarosa, G. (2003). *Adolescent literacy and the achievement gap; What do we know and where do we go from here?* New York: Carnegie Corporation.

Snow, C.E., Burns, M.S., & Griffin, P. (Eds.). (1998). *Preventing reading difficulties in young children.* Washington, DC: National Academies Press.

Spreen, O. (1989). Learning disability, neurology, and long-term outcome: Some implications for the individual and for society. *Journal of Clinical and Experimental Neuropsychology, 11*(3), 389-408.

Stahl, S.A. (1986). Three principles of effective vocabulary instruction. *Journal of Reading, 29*, 662-668.

Stahl, S.A. (1999). *Vocabulary development.* Cambridge, MA: Brookline Books.

Stahl, S.A., & Fairbanks, M. M. (1986). The effects of vocabulary instruction: A model-based meta-analysis. *Review of Educational Research, 56(1),* 72-110.

Stahl, S., & Kapinus, B. (2001). *Word Power: What every educator needs to know about teaching vocabulary.* Washington, DC: National Education Association.

Stahl, S.A. & Kuhn, M.R. (2002). Making it sound like language: Developing fluency. *The Reading Teacher, 55*(6), 582-584.

Stanovich, K.E. (1986). Matthew effects in reading: Some consequences of individual differences in the acquisition of literacy. *Reading Research Quarterly, 21,* 369-407.

References and Further Reading (continued)

Stanovich, K.E. (2000). *Progress in understanding reading: Scientific foundations and new frontiers.* New York: Guilford Press.

Stupski Foundation. (2007). The Secondary Literacy Instruction and Intervention Guide. Mill Valley: CA. Retrieved from http://www.stupski.org/documents/Secondary_Literacy_Instruction_Intervention_Guide.pdf

Swanson, H.L., Hoskyn, M. & Lee, C. (1999). *Intervention for students with learning disabilities: A meta-analysis of treatment outcomes.* New York: The Guilford Press.

Torgesen, J.K. (2005). Essential features of effective reading instruction for struggling readers in grades 4-12. Presented at meetings of the Utah Branch of the International Dyslexia Association. Retrievable from http://www.fcrr.org/science/pdf/torgesen/Utah_remediation.pdf

Torgesen, J.K., & Wagner, R.K. (1987). The nature of phonological processing and its causal role in the acquisition of reading skills. *Psychological Bulletin, 101* 192-212

Torgesen, J.K., & Hudson, R. R., (2006). Reading fluency: Critical issues for struggling readers. In S. J. Samuels & A. E. Parstrup (Eds.), *What research has to say about fluency instruction.* Newark, DE: International Reading Association.

Torgesen, J.K., Houston, D. D., Rissman, L. M., Decker, S. M., Roberts, G., Vaughn, S., et al. (2007). *Academic literacy instruction for adolescents: A guidance document from the Center on Instruction,* Portsmouth, NH: RMC Research Corporation, Center on Instruction.

Vail, P. (1991). *Common ground - Whole language and phonics working together.* Rosemont, NJ: Modern Learning Press.

Vail, P. (1995). *Words fail me - How language works and what happens when it doesn't.* Rosemont, NJ: Modern Learning Press.

Van Cleave, W. (2004). *Everything you want to know and exactly where to find it.* Greenville, S.C.: William Van Cleave.

VanDeWeghe, R., (2009). Engaged learning. Thousand Oaks, CA: Corwin Press.

Vellutino, Frank. (1979). *Dyslexia: Theory and research*. Cambridge: MIT Press.

Velluntino, F.R., Scanlon, D., & Tanzman M. (1994). Component of reading ability: Issues and problems in operationalizing word identification, phonological coding, and orthographic coding. In G. R. Lyon (Ed.), *Frames of Reference for the Assessment of Learning Disabilities: New Views on Measurement Issues.* Baltimore, MD.

Wehmeyer, M.L. (1996). Self-determination as an educational outcome: Why is it important to children, youth, and adults with disabilities? In D.J. Sands & M.L. Wehmeyer (Eds.), *Self-determination Across the Lifespan: Independence and Choice for People with Disabilities* (pp. 17-36). Baltimore: Paul H. Brookes Publishing Co.

References and Further Reading (continued)

Werner, E.E., & Smith, R.S. (1992). *Overcoming the odds: High risk children from birth to adulthood.* Ithaca, NY: Cornell University Press.

West, T. (1997). *In the mind's eye: Visual thinkers, gifted people with dyslexia and other learning difficulties, computer images and the ironies of creativity.* New York: Prometheus Books.

White, T.G., Sowell, J., & Yanagihara, A. (1989). Teaching elementary students to use word-part clues. *Reading Teacher 42,* pp. 302-308

Wilhelm, J. (1996). *"You Gotta BE the Book: Teaching Engaged and Reflective Reading with Adolescents".* New York: Teachers College Press.

Wilson, B.A. (1987). *Wilson study and writing skills.* Oxford, MA: Wilson Language Training.

Wilson, B. (1998). Matching student needs to instruction. S. Reder, & S. Vogel (eds.), *Learning disabilities, literacy and adult education.* Baltimore, MD: Brookes Publishing.

Wilson, B.A. (2003). *Uses of differentiated texts & their interrelationships for students with primary decoding deficits.* Retrieved from http://www.wilsonacademy.com.

Wilson, B. A. (2011). Instruction for older students with a word-level reading disability. In *Multisensory-Teaching of Basic Language Skills* (3rd ed.). Birsh, J. (Ed.), Baltimore, MD: Brookes Publishing Co.

Wilson, B. & Schupack, H. (1997). *Reading, Writing and Spelling – The Multisensory Structured Language Approach.* Baltimore, MD. The International Dyslexia Association.

Wolf, M. (2007). *Proust and the squid: The story and science of the reading brain.* New York: Harper Collins.

NOTES

NOTES

NOTES

NOTES